THAT THESE
DEAD

■ THAT THESE ■
DEAD

KEVIN FLEGLER

TATE PUBLISHING
AND ENTERPRISES, LLC

That These Dead
Copyright © 2015 by Kevin Flegler. All rights reserved.

No part of this publication may be reproduced, stored in a retrieval system or transmitted in any way by any means, electronic, mechanical, photocopy, recording or otherwise without the prior permission of the author except as provided by USA copyright law.

This book is designed to provide accurate and authoritative information with regard to the subject matter covered. This information is given with the understanding that neither the author nor Tate Publishing, LLC is engaged in rendering legal, professional advice. Since the details of your situation are fact dependent, you should additionally seek the services of a competent professional.

The opinions expressed by the author are not necessarily those of Tate Publishing, LLC.

Published by Tate Publishing & Enterprises, LLC
127 E. Trade Center Terrace | Mustang, Oklahoma 73064 USA
1.888.361.9473 | www.tatepublishing.com

Tate Publishing is committed to excellence in the publishing industry. The company reflects the philosophy established by the founders, based on Psalm 68:11,
"The Lord gave the word and great was the company of those who published it."

Book design copyright © 2015 by Tate Publishing, LLC. All rights reserved.
Cover design by Nino Carlo Suico
Interior design by Jomar Ouano

Published in the United States of America

ISBN: 978-1-68187-214-8
1. History / United States / Civil War Period (1850-1877)
2. History / Military / World War II
15.09.17

To my family. Thank you for your sacrifice and service throughout the war in Iraq and Afghanistan, at home, and abroad. I'm proud of you. Our nation is indebted to you, and all those who have defended America since 9/11.

To my dad. Thank you for your service and the example of patriotism you have displayed in life.

To every American who has defended this nation in and out of uniform throughout our nation's history. America would not exist without their selfless sacrifice. May we continue to follow their example, preserving liberty and freedom for generations to come.

Contents

Introduction 9
Prologue 13

1 The Nature of War 21
2 Saving Lives 65
    Be Prepared 66
    Act before a Crisis 76
    Clearly Define Realistic Objectives 84
    Act Decisively 94
    Prosecute War Aggressively 101
    Persevere 113
3 Learning from History 121

Epilogue 189
Notes 193

Introduction

...Shall Not Have Died in Vain

Something stirs within the heart of every patriotic American when they see the flag flutter in the breeze or the color guard pass in a parade. It is a stirring of loyalty, devotion, and pride. Pride in a nation that idealizes equality, liberty, and freedom. And it is to those ideals that there is a sense of loyalty and devotion. Presidential administrations come and go. Congress changes every two years; some are better, some are worse than others in how they reflect through law the ideals they are sworn to uphold and represent. Loyalty to the government, embodied through the president and Congress, is often given out of a sense of duty. But loyalty to the flag and the ideals it represents of sacrifice, equality, liberty, and freedom is given with a heart of love. America is not a president or Congress. America is an idea expressed in the Declaration of Independence and codified in the Constitution. That is where patriotic loyalty lies.

Something also stirs within the hearts of patriotic Americans when they see a soldier in uniform. It is a stirring of gratitude and thankfulness, for the idea of America cannot continue without the sacrifice of the men and women who protect these shores. The sound of "Taps" produces gut-wrenching emotions, from overwhelming grief to euphoria, for that sound signifies the death of a loyal hero who served or fell in service to country. There is grief at the loss of a patriot but euphoria from the courage, honor, duty, devotion, and love for country their life represented. That sound is also a call, a call to everyone who hears to follow in the example of the deceased and stand in defense of the flag. It is a call that is answered in heart. The patriotic of every age and gender raise their hand and say, "I will go." Any outside invader of America would not just face the military in uniform but an army of loyal patriots willing to die for the ideals of equality, liberty, and freedom.

There is another stirring in patriots. But this is the stirring of an ember, an ember that becomes a hot glowing coal of anger. Anger against a political establishment that, at times, makes military decisions based on their own political benefit. An establishment that sends American soldiers into battle without the equipment they need because they are concerned about how the appearance of American might will be perceived by the rest of the world. An establishment that appears more concerned with the welfare of America's enemies than the welfare of America's soldiers. Frankly, an establishment that acts clueless to the realities of the evil world we live in and ignorant of the nature of war. And an establishment that gives the military vague, vacillating, unrealistic, or unattainable objectives. All of this results in the loss of American lives and leaves patriotic citizens asking the question why.

It is up to us, patriotic citizens, to put political pressure on our elected officials to make wise decisions about the use of our military. This book provides a foundation for citizens to articulate and demand our political leadership to do this. It provides a standard by which American war policy can be measured and politicians can be held accountable for their decisions. I believe the sacrifice of our men and women in uniform should be held in the highest regard. Their lives are precious, and they need us, patriotic Americans, to watch their back on the home front. They need us to defend them from policies that risk their lives senselessly. They need us to make sure no life is lost in vain.

Four score and seven years ago our fathers brought forth on this continent, a new nation, conceived in Liberty, and dedicated to the proposition that all men are created equal.

Now we are engaged in a great civil war, testing whether that nation, or any nation so conceived and so dedicated, can long endure. We are met on a great battle-field of that war. We have come to dedicate a portion of that field, as a final resting place for those who here gave their lives that that nation might live. It is altogether fitting and proper that we should do this.

But, in a larger sense, we can not dedicate—we can not consecrate—we cannot hallow—this ground. The brave men, living and dead, who struggled here, have consecrated it, far above our poor power to add or detract. The world will little note, nor long remember what we say here, but it can never forget what they did here. It is for us the living, rather, to be dedicated here to the unfinished work which they who fought here have thus far so nobly advanced. It is rather for us to be here dedicated to the great task remaining before us—that from these honored dead we take increased devotion to that cause for which they gave the last full measure of devotion—that we here highly resolve that these dead shall not have died in vain—that this nation, under God, shall have a new birth of freedom—and that government of the people, by the people, for the people, shall not perish from the earth.

> Abraham Lincoln's "Gettysburg Address"
> November 19, 1863

Prologue

His eyes squinted as he stepped out into the sunlight, and a wave of dizziness threatened to overcome him. He reached out for the porch railing to steady himself, slowly so as not to raise any suspicions among the crowd gathered in front of Mr. Wills's house that he wasn't feeling well. He wasn't sure what was causing his present discomfort. He had started to feel fatigued yesterday on the train. Not that fatigue was an unusual companion. The war was now in its third year. At times, it seemed that the war and its unending difficulties was all he had known: preserving the Union, slavery, emancipation, political fighting, and finding a general that understood how to prosecute this war.[1]

A flash of anger shot through him along with that last thought: finding a general. The most recent in a long line and the current officer appointed as commander of the Army of the Potomac was Major General George Gordon Meade, and he had disappointed Mr. Lincoln as well. He remembered the frustrating days after the news that Lee's army had been defeated at Gettysburg. He had telegraphed General Meade, urging him to pursue and destroy Lee's battered army. Even the weather seemed to be aiding the Union with rains swelling the Potomac and temporarily trapping the Confederates in the North. But there wasn't an attack. General Meade was content with the victory at Gettysburg, and Lee slipped back to the safety of Virginia. Meade offered his resignation for disappointing the president, and in great anger the president wrote a letter explaining how the failure to destroy Lee's army had prolonged the war, but as he had done so many times before with other generals, or in similar situations, he never sent the letter. Instead he expressed his gratitude for what was accomplished and decided to wait for the right moment, and right person, to replace General Meade. No, better to be patient than rash. He remembered his words to those who wanted him to alter his emancipation proclamation: "I am a slow walker, but I never walk back."[2]

The cheering and applause of the crowd jolted him back to the present from his thoughts, and he straightened himself. The sunlight did feel good, and the dampness from the earlier showers that had passed through made the air fresh. It was a beautiful day for November, and the crowd formed a procession to move out to the cemetery for the dedication. He thought of Mary as they moved along. She was worried about him making this trip. Tad had fallen ill, and the struggles with handling Willie's death made Mary anxious for Tad. She was still deeply saddened as well over the death of her brother-in-law, Ben Hardin Helm, and worried about her sister Emilie. Ben had fallen fighting for the Confederacy at Chickamauga. Mary's family had been hit hard by the war. Three half-brothers had been killed, all fighting for the cause he was attempting to put down. But many families had been hit hard, and the nation itself was torn in two.

That is why he had to make the trip. He didn't usually accept invitations to speak. But when David Wills had sent the invitation early in the month to speak at the dedication of the new Soldiers' National Cemetery, he thought it would be an important opportunity to put what had taken place at Gettysburg in July in perspective. It was still going to be a long war; General Meade had unknowingly sealed that by letting Lee escape. Somehow, he had to strengthen the resolve of the Union for what was still ahead. He had to convey the importance of what was being fought for. But how could he? He hadn't been able to convince his generals about the nature of this war. Meade had triumphantly rejoiced over driving Lee from Union soil. Others had boasted to Lincoln of laying siege to Richmond. Why didn't they understand this war was to have one nation established upon equality and freedom, and the greatest obstacle to that at the moment was Lee's army? There could be no compromise, no settlement, no satisfaction with keeping Lee in Virginia or the symbolic capture of a city. Anything less than one free nation would be failure.

In the days and weeks since the invitation, he had given much thought to what he would say. When he looked at the casualty reports, the task became more daunting. They were staggering numbers. Over seven thousand lay dead on the field. Over twenty-seven thousand were wounded and maimed, many of whom would suffer horribly for months before succumbing to death. Still thousands more were missing and unaccounted for.[3] Is it possible to justify such horror? What words could he say that would make sense of what happened and be an encouragement to continue on? He had to content himself with the fact that the words he had prepared conveyed his heart and belief; it would be up to Providence to make the nation understand.

At the podium, the start of the ceremony was delayed while everyone waited for Mr. Edward Everett to arrive. He had been walking the battlefield to get inspiration for his address. The president was eager to meet Mr. Everett, for he had a very distinguished career. He was a Harvard graduate, who later taught Greek literature there. He had been a congressman, governor, president of Harvard, the secretary of state, and a senator.

Mr. Everett was expected to give a lengthy address, and as he did, the president looked out over the crowd of at least fifteen thousand, a small gathering compared to the 170,000 men who had clashed here in July. Would this current gathering understand what the war was about or what the significance of the summer's battle had been? The mood of the crowd the night before had been festive, celebratory. In one sense, he could understand the jubilation. The north had suffered plenty of bloody defeats with Fredericksburg and Chancellorsville in the past year. Even he had been elated when news came of the almost-simultaneous victories at Vicksburg and Gettysburg. But after the initial relief the news of these victories brought, the realization returned that the war still had an indefinite ending. What effect would that realization have on the Union? Would the people become weary of war and press for peace, content that Union troops had evened the score? Yes, that was his fear. That was the reason he had made this trip. If the Union turned back now, if any terms of peace were accepted other than one free, united nation, then what had it all been for? What did the blood-soaked ground , the screams of the wounded, the cries of grief stricken families mean? His heart sank from the weight of these thoughts, from the image of the ground before him strewn with the dead. *Resolve*. That was the word that would carry him through. Resolve. That is what the Union must have. Resolve that the death of the men on this field, and every other field thus far, was not without purpose. Resolve that this war would be carried on to a victorious end. Resolve that these dead shall not have died in vain.

Fallujah, Iraq, March 31, 2004. Iraqi insurgents kill and mutilate the bodies of four civilian contractors. Throughout the month of April that year, coalition forces conducted operations within the city in response to the killings, but at the request of the Iraqi governing authorities, they withdrew from the city in early May.

During the summer of 2004, insurgents strengthened their position in the city. On November 7, 2004, Operation Phantom Fury began to rid Fallujah of insurgents and establish the security of the city. The six-week campaign that followed was the bloodiest operation of the Iraq war. By December 23, an estimated 1,200 insurgents had been killed. The US Marines, who took the lead in the offensive, suffered seventy killed in action and 651 wounded.[4] Total coalition deaths numbered around one hundred. For the Marines, it was the deadliest fighting since the Vietnam War, and the battle itself holds a place among the historic and momentous actions of the Corps.[5]

Yet less than ten years after Operation Phantom Fury, Fallujah is back in the hands of an enemy with roots to the same insurgents driven out in 2004.[6] IS (Islamic State) is led by the man who was once the leader of al-Qaida in Iraq, Abu Bakr al-Baghdadi. IS, as it is currently labeled, started as al-Qaida in Iraq. But as it has grown and absorbed other extremist groups and conquered territory, its name has changed: first to ISIL (Islamic State of Iraq and the Levant), then to ISIS (Islamic State in Iraq and Syria), to IS.[7]

This is just another sad chapter in America's war history of the last sixty years. A history filled with unfinished victories, lost American lives, questions as to why wars were even fought, and politicians who lack the resolve of President Lincoln to see a war brought to true victory and the determination that no American life will be lost in vain.

Major General Lawrence Nicholson of the First Marine Division stated concerning the fall of Fallujah back into extremist hands: "Our tagline for this has always been: We did our job, we did it well and we'll just leave it at that."[8] But a former sergeant was much more blunt, echoing the sentiments of many Americans when he told *The New York Times*: "It made me sick to my stomach to have that thrown in our face, everything we fought for so blatantly taken away."[9] America's military does do its job well, and Americans are proud of their soldiers. But Americans are also tired of that sick feeling that comes when the blood and effort of their brave soldiers are squandered by poor policy and weak resolve. It's time for a change.

1

The Nature of War

Why is humanity fascinated by war? Movies are produced, books are written, and songs are sung about war. Some of these portray the human tragedy, others glorify the action, some tell an individual's story, and some proffer a hero. But who determines who is a hero? And what actions are determined to be heroic? Is a hero simply a propaganda tool put forth to encourage others to rally to a cause? Or are there genuine character qualities that societies refer to as heroic, which are the best qualities of humans, not normally displayed? Children act out war in their play. Video games about war are played by child and adult alike. Toys are made of the instruments of war. Humanity is fascinated by war.

This human attachment to war is one of the great paradoxes of life. It seems strange that war, which involves the destruction of human life, is honored and glorified by so many. If the sanctity of human life is a virtue of civilized society, then why would war that involves the destruction of human life be glorified?

This fascination and glorification of war is often not on the minds of those who experience its horrors. Ernie Pyle, the famed and honored World War II correspondent, was killed by Japanese machine gun fire on the island of Ie Shima April 18, 1945.[10] During the war, he had reported from London, Africa, and throughout the European theater. He was greatly beloved by the troops whose story he told and the audience that read his columns. He wrote of the horror and suffering he witnessed and the men who died next to him, and he hated war. At one point, he had to leave the front, saying, "I don't think I could go on and keep sane."[11] But his sense of duty and devotion to the troops drew him back to the battle, this time in the Pacific theater, where he died telling the story of the sacrifices being made there. Of the soldiers he loved, he wrote, "In their eyes as they pass is not hatred, not excitement, not despair, not the tonic of their victory. There is just the simple expression of being there as if they had been doing that forever, and nothing else."[12]

John Hersey was a magazine journalist who followed the marines on Guadalcanal. He wrote a book about one of the battles he witnessed titled *Into the Valley*. He recounts a conversation with the Marines about what was happening in other theaters of the war and their own situation, and he asks them what they were fighting for. Faces became sullen and troubled. After a seemingly long pause, one of the men whispers, "Jesus, what I'd give for a piece of blueberry pie."[13] Others began whispering their own personal preference for a particular flavor of pie. What does pie have to do with reasons for fighting a war? Hersey explains that to these men "pie" was a symbol of home. They were fighting for home. And therein lies part of the answer to why humanity honors and glorifies war. *There are principles, values, and institutions that transcend the value of human life*. Defending home and family is one of them.

Often, war is an embodiment of the struggle between good and evil. On a personal level, every person struggles with the definition of what is good or what is evil. There is a struggle to carry out what is determined to be good. The struggle of defining and acting on what is good extends to societies as well. Though it is puzzling to some why the instinct and recognition of good and evil exists within man, it is undeniable that it is there. Along with the instinct that good exists is a belief that what is good is the better choice. When wars present a clear distinction between good and evil, nations and men are willing to stand and fight for what is good, and society honors that.

But there is a paradox in that distinction between good and evil as well. For what one nation or culture considers good, another may consider evil. Perhaps no war in American history presented such a clear distinction between good and evil as the Second World War. Imperial Japan was waging a war of aggression to expand its empire, Nazi Germany was waging a war of subjugation to establish their theory of the master race, yet there were those in both Japan and Germany who believed in the good of what they were doing. Sometimes the distinctions are not as pronounced.

In large part, the value system of a nation and their determination of good and evil are directly related to the cultural view of the value of human life. America has an expressed statement for the basis of good in the Declaration of Independence. "We hold these truths to be self-evident: That all men are created equal; that they are endowed by their Creator with certain unalienable rights; that among these are life, liberty, and the pursuit of happiness." That is also a value statement of the worth placed upon human life. The belief in the equality of all men is essential to the concept of liberty. Freedom is the liberty to possess and express individual rights. But rights do not exist without a belief in the equality of all men, that every individual has an equal claim to life, to the liberty to use their gifts and talents for the procurement of their own needs, and to retain the ownership of what is produced by their efforts for their own happiness. Without a belief in the equality of all men, which imperial Japan and Nazi Germany rejected, rights simply become privileges granted by the powerful. Lest it be thought that Japan and Germany are the only nations that have failed to recognize the equality of all humanity, it's good to remember that America wrestled with the issue from its founding through the Civil War in regard to slavery and still wrestles with recognizing that an unborn child is a human being. But as nations step forward to recognize the equality of men and fight to preserve the rights of men, another of the values that transcend life is defended. Good triumphs over evil, and it is right to glory in that.

Almost all men value their own life. The instinct of self-preservation is strong. Self-sacrifice is against what comes natural to man. In war, self-sacrifice is often on display, and it has a spellbinding effect on those who see it. Hearts are stirred with admiration for it, and hearts wonder if they would have the same level of devotion for another. Self-sacrifice is truly one of the better human character qualities not normally displayed that can be called heroic. Jesus said, "Greater love has no one than this, than to lay down one's life for his friends."[14] When war is conducted for a just cause, every life laid down is a demonstration of the greatest love humans can express. Even when the cause is not clear and the soldier at the front can't articulate the reason why he is there, the person next to him is all the reason he needs to lay down his life. There is a holy and awe-inspiring fascination with that.

Edward Everett walked the fields of Gettysburg before his oration that November day in 1863. In his speech, he made this comment: "I feel, as never before, how justly, from the dawn of history to the present time, men have paid the homage of their gratitude and admiration to the memory of those who nobly sacrifice their lives, that their fellowmen may live in safety and in honor."[15]

Courage is another of the heroic character qualities displayed in war that is worthy of honor. While self-sacrifice is giving up life or well-being for another, courage is a demonstration of the willingness to do so. Courage is often fueled by devotion and loyalty, and it is thought of in expressions of daring. But in reality, courage is displayed by every soldier who fulfills his duty, and the honor that should be shown to every soldier is a tribute to his or her courage. Incidents that demonstrate actions beyond the normal duties of war are often awarded and remembered. One such incident occurred on December 13, 1862.

Major John Pelham was a twenty-four-year-old artillerist serving the Confederacy in J. E. B. Stuart's horse artillery. During the Battle of Fredericksburg, Stuart and his artillery were positioned on the right flank of the Confederate line. On the morning of December 13, approximately fifty-five thousand Union troops were in position to assault that line, defended by Stonewall Jackson's corp. As the federal troops began their advance, young Major Pelham moved two artillery pieces forward and commenced an enfilade upon them. Despite the Union turning a division of infantry and several batteries of their own artillery to silence Pelham's pieces, through quick movements and unrelenting fire, Major Pelham halted the Union advance for over an hour. It wasn't until he was ordered by Stuart with the words, "Get back from destruction, you infernal, gallant fool, John Pelham," that he returned to the safety of his own lines.[16] General Lee, regarding the incident, commented, "It is glorious to see such courage in one so young."[17]

Another incident, at the conclusion of the Civil War, illustrates the admiration and honor held for courage, devotion, and loyalty. After General Lee's surrender to General Grant at Appomattox, the Confederate troops were required to stack their arms before disbanding. The following account shows the deep emotion and respect these virtues deserve:

> A gallant color-bearer, as he delivered up the tattered remnant of his flag, burst into tears and said to the Federal soldiers who received it, "Boys, this is not the first time you have seen that flag. I have borne it in the very forefront of the battle on many a victorious field, and I had rather die than surrender it now." "Brave fellow," said General Chamberlain, of Maine, who heard the remark, "I admire your noble spirit, and only regret that I have not the authority to bid you keep your flag and carry it home as a precious heirloom."[18]

Courage isn't just displayed in battle or in fulfilling duty; it is also displayed in acts of compassion and care. Pulling a fallen comrade from danger and giving care to the wounded are acts of courage that are honorable and glorious as well. Richard Kirkland was a sergeant serving in the Second South Carolina Regiment. During the same battle at Fredericksburg that Major Pelham served so valiantly, Mr. Kirkland and the Second South Carolina were positioned on the Confederate left, entrenched behind a stone wall. Their position was virtually impenetrable. But wave after wave of Union troops were thrown against it. The casualties were horrific. The suffering of the wounded men in front of him so touched Richard that he asked permission to leave the line and offer aid to the fallen enemy. Permission was granted, and he put himself at risk to carry water and do whatever else he could for the wounded. He was honored with the appellation "the humane hero of Fredericksburg."[19] This is another example of the great paradoxes in war. At one moment, the trigger is pulled to take the life of an enemy, and the next, the same soldier is risking his life to save the same enemy.

These paradoxes are only explainable and understandable within the criterion of a worldview that recognizes the equality of man and value of human life but also believes there are principals, values, and institutions that are of greater value than life. Under that rubric, the actions of war that have been explained can be honorable and glorious: defending home, preserving liberty, destroying evil, self-sacrifice, courage, loyalty, and devotion to a righteous cause. It is possible to kill without hatred. To fight only to stop the enemy and then show love, care, and compassion to him, as did Richard Kirkland. This worldview was alluded to by Patrick Henry in his famous speech before the Second Virginia Convention on March 23, 1775, when he asked, "Is life so dear, or peace so sweet, as to be purchased at the price of chains and slavery?"

His answer "Give me liberty or give me death!" demonstrated his belief in a value that transcends life.

Despite these values that are worthy of honor and glory and that fascinate humanity, war remains a horrible event to be avoided, but that isn't always possible. Just as there are evil men in society, so there are evil societies, cultures, and nations. Nazi Germany and imperial Japan have already been mentioned as familiar examples, but many more could be given, and many more exist today. There is an evil side of mankind that glorifies pride and power, that does not believe in the equality of humanity. There is also a sadistic element in mankind that takes pleasure in destroying life. Understanding these evil components, along with the values discussed previously, forms a basis to determine the virtue of the media a society produces about war and the virtue of a society's fascination with war.

The complexities of the reasons why wars exist, the paradoxes that are evident in war, and its unavoidability are aptly seen in the American Civil War, and within that, the Battle of Fredericksburg is a microcosm. The Battle of Fredericksburg took place between December 11 and 15, 1862. This was shortly before the second anniversary of South Carolina's vote to secede from the Union, December 20, 1860, and twenty months after the beginning of hostilities at Fort Sumter, April 12, 1861.

During that twenty-month interval, the nation had seen many costly battles with victories for both sides that had resulted in very little change in the overall situation between the North and South. The primary strategy for the North had been to make an advance upon Richmond, the Confederate Capital, in the hope that the Confederate army would be drawn out into battle to defend the city and be destroyed by superior Union forces while the South employed a defensive strategy with, at times, brilliant counterattacks to repel the Union army.

The first large-scale battle of the Civil War occurred July 21, 1861, after Union forces commanded by General Irwin McDowell had marched south of Washington to take control of a crucial railroad junction known as Manassa's Gap, or Manassa's Junction, named after a man, Manassa, who had previously settled in the area.[20] This battle is called either First Manassas, or Battle of Bull Run, after the small stream that runs three miles north of the junction. The battle pitched back and forth throughout the day but eventually ended in the panicked retreat of federal troops back to Washington. As a result, General McDowell was replaced by General George McClellan.

McClellan was small in stature but large in ego. However, his personality and organizational skills were an asset to the Union at this time. It was General McClellan who took the waves of new recruits flooding to the Union cause in the Washington area and formed them into a confident, disciplined, and equipped fighting force. During the fall of 1861 and winter of 1862, he amassed an army of over one hundred thousand designated as the Army of the Potomac but was reluctant to use it. Finally in the spring of 1862, after many urgings by the president, McClellan submitted a plan to move on Richmond once again. This operation is known as the Peninsula Campaign and entailed landing the army on the Virginia peninsula between the York and James Rivers and marching up the peninsula to lay siege to Richmond. The reluctance of General McClellan to use his army continued even after the plan was in place. He was overly cautious, greatly overestimated the strength of the Confederate forces opposing him, and slow to move. A small Confederate force at Yorktown flustered the general into taking a month to put a siege in place around the city. The South used this time to increase the troop strength and defenses around Richmond, and then the defenders of Yorktown simply withdrew. McClellan slowly pushed up the peninsula toward Richmond. At the end of June 1862, Confederate forces launched a series of attacks on McClellan's force. The Seven Days Battles, as they are known, were costly on both sides. And although the Union army held the line overall, McClellan withdrew his army south to the James River and set up in a defensive position. He was convinced again that he faced overwhelming odds and made pleas to Washington for reinforcements. By August, President Lincoln knew McClellan wasn't going to mount an offensive and ordered him to bring his forces back from Harrison's Landing on the James River to Washington. The Army of the Potomac was once again encamped on the banks of the Potomac.

During the time McClellan's forces were on the peninsula, the Union army of Virginia had been organized under Major General John Pope. Confederate General Lee, upon seeing McClellan entrenched at Harrison's Landing, had turned his forces north again from Richmond. At the end of August, with McClellan's forces just returning from the peninsula, a fierce battle was again fought at Manassas. Referred to as Second Manassas, or Second Battle of Bull Run, the Confederate army defeated Pope. McClellan had been hesitant to go to the aid of Pope, squabbling over who would have command of the joint Army of Virginia and Army of the Potomac. Although the president was angry over McClellan's arrogance, he relieved Pope of his command and combined the rest of his army under McClellan's command with the Army of the Potomac.

Now at the beginning of September 1862, General Lee, who commanded the Army of Northern Virginia for the Confederacy, made a bold decision to invade the North via Maryland. It was an attempt to shift the battle away from the state of Virginia, gain a victory on Union soil, demoralize the North, and gain foreign recognition. The leadership of the Confederacy recognized the superiority of the North's capability to prosecute the war. Robert Lewis Dabney, who served on the staff of General Thomas "Stonewall" Jackson and wrote a contemporary biography of him, wrote concerning this superiority:

> To fight this battle, eleven millions,...prepared to meet twenty millions. The gigantic adversary was not impeded by distance, but lay everywhere alongside his proposed victim, ready to grasp him with his long arms. He held prepared, a veteran army of twenty thousand men, a navy, and vast arsenals and armories; while the Confederate States had everything to create. He had the administration of all the departments of a government; he had revenues, a treasury recruited perpetually with the gold of the modern Ophir, and huge accumulations of financial wealth: they had none. In his favor was a great commercial marine, second to none in the world, and manufactories teeming with productive labor...; while she had agricultural communities, possessing only the rudiments of commerce and of the arts.[21]

Given these considerations, the South's strategy wasn't to gain a military victory that would impose the Confederate Constitution upon all the states but to prolong and make the war costly enough to the North that they would become weary of fighting and sue for peace, recognizing the independence of the Confederate states from the Union. Thus, General Lee, confident from the Confederate victories over the past year and convinced of the lack of desire for the Union armies to fight, moved into Maryland to facilitate those ends.

What General Lee did not expect was General McClellan's quick movements and aggressive tactics. In part, McClellan was emboldened by captured dispatches that reveled the position of the Confederates, but also, men fight with greater determination when they are defending their own soil. On September 17, 1862, the armies clashed between Antietam Creek and Sharpsburg. It was the bloodiest day of fighting in the Civil War and American history, with approximately six thousand dead and another seventeen thousand wounded.[22] Other battles yet to come would produce greater casualties over several days, but this horrific total was for a single day of fighting. Lee's men were driven back from their original emplacement. On the eighteenth, both armies remained in their positions, unwilling to continue the fight. That night, the Confederate forces slipped back across the Potomac into Virginia; and McClellan, content with stopping Lee's invasion, let him retreat.

The president was disappointed and disgusted that McClellan hadn't followed up on his victory by pursuing General Lee. Throughout October, the Army of the Potomac remained encamped while Lincoln continued to urge McClellan to resume the offensive. At one point, he ordered McClellan to march between Lee's army and Richmond saying that the Union troops could fight and march "as well as the enemy" and "it is unmanly to say they can not do it."[23] But McClellan refused. As of October 25, when he still hadn't broke camp, he reported to the president that his horses were too tired to move. To which the president replied, "Will you pardon me for asking what the horses of your army have done since the battle of Antietam that fatigue anything?"[24] By the first part of November, President Lincoln had had enough of McClellan's procrastination and fired him. He appointed Ambrose E. Burnside to command the Army of the Potomac. Ambrose Burnside was known for his bushy sideburns. He had commanded part of the Union forces that had been successful at Antietam. The stage was now set for the Battle of Fredericksburg.

Fredericksburg is located on the south side of the Rappahannock River in northeastern Virginia. An offensive into the South through Fredericksburg offered several advantages to the army under General Burnside. Unlike the Peninsula Campaign, this route would keep the Army of the Potomac in front of Washington, thereby protecting it. A direct rail line connected Richmond to Fredericksburg of sixty miles in length, giving Union troops an avenue to advance and be supplied as they went. Railways connected the Potomac and Rappahannock and the river itself could be used as a supply line.

As the large and cumbersome Union army of nearly 130,000 men advanced toward Fredericksburg in late November 1862, the Confederate army was moving into positions on the south side of the Rappahannock. A crucial delay in the arrival of pontoons for Burnside's army to cross the river, allowed the Confederates to mass their forces in defensive positions before the Union could get across the river and take up positions on the heights south of Fredericksburg. Between those heights and the river lay a fertile plain through which a road and railroad tracks ran. The heights form a shape similar to half of an ellipse with the river cutting the center and descend into the plain east of town some three to four miles. It was along these heights that the Confederate forces took up their positions. On the north side of the river, the Union army was encamped, protected by an impressive number of cannon placed along the Stafford Heights behind them.

On December 11, Union troops began to cross the river. One mile east of town, a stream called Deep Run emptied into the Rappahannock. Here, a steep incline close to the river on the south side, as well as the cannons behind them, allowed the Union army to cross the river unmolested. At Fredericksburg, however, Barksdale's brigade of Confederate soldiers had taken up position inside the town and delayed the Union crossing most of the day. This delaying action had allowed General Lee to make his final adjustments to the Confederate defenses. The weather on the twelfth covered the river valley in fog and allowed the Union army to fully cross the river and take up their offensive positions behind the road. The morning of the thirteenth opened in fog, but by ten o'clock, it began to lift, revealing the sea of blue soldiers before the Confederate lines, poised to make their assault. General Burnside's plan was to make simultaneous assaults at the right and left of the Confederate line. The Confederate right was commanded by General Jackson and offered the best chance of success for the Union as the heights at this end began their decent into the plain. It was during the first charge by the Union on the right that Major Pelham made his heroic stance with his artillery. This first charge was repelled, but another assault was made after noon that reached a marshy wooded area protruding out from the Confederate line. Fierce and close combat ensued in the woods, and again, the Confederate defenders drove the federal troops back. Another assault was made on the inside right when Union troops used the cover of Deep Run to advance close to the Confederate line, but this ended in a Union retreat as well.

On the left end of the Confederate line, near the town of Fredericksburg, the defenders had taken up positions behind the stone wall along the main road heading south out of Fredericksburg as it made its bend around the base of Marye's Hill. Upon that hill and the heights beyond it, Confederate artillery was placed to cover the approach of the plain. It was an extremely strong defensive position. Against this impregnable wall, General Burnside ordered six futile charges that produced such an appalling slaughter of his men that the plain was "literally encumbered with corpses."[25] Many of the survivors of those charges fled into the town of Fredericksburg for shelter, and others caught out in front of the wall tried to find shelter in any depression or behind the bodies of their fallen comrades.

The Confederate generals expected renewed assaults on the fourteenth, and General Burnside wanted to push the issue, but his subordinate commanders balked at the prospect of charging into the Southern defenses again. So the day of the fourteenth passed without hostilities, except for the occasional exchange of artillery and sharpshooters. During the day on the fifteenth, a truce was requested by the Union so they might recover their dead and wounded from the fighting of the thirteenth. Some of these wounded had spent two days suffering, lying on the frozen ground.

General Burnside now found his army in a difficult situation. They were unable to advance from the safety of their entrenchment along the road, and they were unable to retreat back across the river without the Confederates attacking while they were in a defenseless position. In chess terms, the Union army was in check and the Confederates had high hopes of bringing about a checkmate. The night of the fifteenth brought an unexpected opportunity for the Union as strong rain and wind blew in from the south. With the darkness to hide their movements and the favorable wind and rain to conceal the noise, the Union army slipped back across the river throughout the night, in spots propping corpses up as fake sentries to fool the Confederate sentries.

The Battle of Fredericksburg had been a crushing defeat for the Union. Union casualties were 12,631 in dead and wounded while Confederate losses were 5,322.[26] The Union was fortunate to escape with the army intact. Both Generals

Lee and Jackson expressed their disappointment over the lost opportunity to bring a greater defeat over the Union and possibly end the war. The Union had been trapped. General Jackson had reconnoitered the field after the events of the thirteenth, looking for a weakness to attack, believing the Union troops had lost the desire to continue the fight, but the road gave the Union a strong defensive position. They were only vulnerable if they advanced or retreated from it. R. L. Dabney gave this summary of Lee's view of Burnside's retreat: "His beaten enemy had again extricated himself from a situation, which promised a complete triumph and a speedy peace to the Confederacy."[27] This view underscores the objective of the Confederacy to reach a peace that would recognize the independence of the Confederacy from the Union.

One paradox of war displayed during the Battle of Fredericksburg has already been recounted in the story of Sergeant Richard Kirkland, the humane hero of Fredericksburg. It is also interesting and seems odd that during the truce on the fifteenth, this description was recorded:

> [G]rim-visaged war now smoothed its horrors for a few hours; and while the hospital attendants were busy in removing the dead and wounded, officers and men from the adverse ranks mingled together in familiar intercourse.[28]

Those who had been engaged in killing one another a couple of days before were now mingling and casually talking together on the same field. This not only illustrates a paradox but is an illustration of the complexities about why wars are fought. The American Civil War was a war in which deeply held convictions, valued more than life, caused families and friends who loved each other to take up arms against each other for the cause they valued while retaining the love for their friend and brother. From the first lady's family to Generals Lewis Armistead and Winfield Scott Hancock, whose lives played out like a surreal divine tragedy, to the privates on the line, the war was fought by some men who held irreconcilable convictions without malice.

Armistead and Hancock were beloved friends who parted in the spring of 1861 to lead men on opposite sides in the coming war. In the climactic point of the entire war, Pickett's Charge at Gettysburg, the two friends faced each other for the first and last time on the field. General Armistead and a few heroic survivors of the Confederate charge breached the stone wall and advanced to take a cannon but were quickly cut down by a Union counterattack. Armistead wounded but alive asked for his old friend Hancock, whose Second Corps was defending the point, only to find out he had been wounded as well. General Armistead died of his wounds on July 5, but General Hancock recovered. Some reports claim that Lewis Armistead had sent a package to Almira Hancock, the general's wife, to be opened in the event of Lewis's death. It was his personal Bible. Perhaps that is just an embellishment of an earlier event in which he gave his personal prayer book to her at their parting in California. But there is no questioning the love and devotion between General Armistead and the Hancock family. Such stories seem hard to understand. What convictions would prompt loving friends and good men to take up arms against each other? That question may best be answered by looking at the service of one of Americas most beloved and respected generals, Robert Edward Lee.

From the center of the Confederate lines on December 13, General Lee watched as the Union assaults on the right were repulsed, and the waves of Union troops hurling themselves against the defenders behind the stone wall at Fredericksburg were cut down. He remarked, "It is well that this is so terrible, or else we might grow fond of it."[29] What was there to be fond of in all the slaughter just witnessed? He was not referring to the slaughter itself, but the duty, courage, loyalty, devotion, honor, and self-sacrifice that he had just witnessed.

Robert E. Lee was a man held in the highest respects by the men of his day. He was known for his devotion to duty, humility, simplicity, gentleness, self-denial for the good of others, quiet dignity, and devout Christian faith.[30] One critic, describing his patience with his subordinate officers, said his "nature was too epicene to be purely a military man."[31] In a letter to his wife on June 5, 1839, he expresses his great care for his children.

> I hope you are all well and will continue so; and therefore must again urge you to be very prudent and careful of those dear children. If I could only get a

squeeze at that little fellow turning up his sweet mouth to 'keeze Baba!' You must not let him run wild in my absence, and will have to exercise firm authority over all of them. This will not require severity, or even strictness, but constant attention, and an unwavering course. Mildness and forbearance, tempered by firmness and judgment, will strengthen their affection for you, while it will maintain your control over them.[32]

The pleasantries between General Grant and General Lee at the surrender at Appomattox are well-known, but many old comrades that became foes quickly became comrades again and showed their respect for General Lee at the surrender. General Gordon Meade, who commanded the Army of the Potomac from Gettysburg to the war's end, had served with Lee before the war. The two had a friendly visit at camp around Appomattox in which Lee jested, "Meade, years are telling on you; your hair is getting quite gray." Meade replied, "Ah, General Lee, it is not the work of years; you are responsible for my gray hairs."[33] General Hunt also met with Lee and gives this record of their meeting.

> He looked, of course, weary and careworn, but in this supreme hour was the same self-possessed, dignified gentleman that I had always known him.…I took my leave, asking General Lee how General Long was and where I would find him.…Long had been a lieutenant in my battery before the war and we were old friends.

> This was the last time I saw General Lee—a truly great man, as great in adversity as in prosperity.[34]

Robert Edward Lee died on October 12, 1870. Many tributes were given by his beloved soldiers he cared so deeply for, and newspapers throughout the North extolled and eulogized a great man. Two excerpts from New York newspapers typify the sentiments expressed by many.

From the *New York Sun*: "in the death of General Lee an able soldier, a sincere Christian, and an honest man has been taken from earth."

And from the *New York Herald*: "In him the military genius of America was developed to a greater extent than ever before. In him all that was pure and lofty in mind and purpose found lodgment. He came nearer the ideal of a soldier and Christian general than any man we can think of, for he was a greater soldier then Havelock, and equally as devout a Christian."[35]

The true character of a man isn't always what the world sees but what the man is in his private life. Reading the private letters of General Lee, throughout his life, to family, friends, and brothers in arms, reveal he was indeed that rare man who truly was what the world saw him to be.

At the suggestion of the aged General Winfield Scott, President Lincoln offered field command of the Union army to Lee at the outset of the war. Lee refused. Francis Preston Blair was Lincoln's liaison to Lee. Lee told Mr. Blair "that if the four millions of slaves in the South belonged to him he would free them with a stroke of his pen to avert the war, —yet as the war had actually begun and he must decide on which side he would draw his sword he could not hesitate— he could not fight against his native State, his home, and his children."[36] Robert Lee was devoted to preserving the Union but ultimately felt his greater duty was to his state, Virginia. Of all other considerations concerning secession and slavery, his actions were driven by a sense of duty to his state. The views he expressed concerning the former demonstrate how highly he regarded duty as a virtue. In a letter to his wife, December 27, 1856, he made these remarks regarding slavery:

> In this enlightened age there are few, I believe, but will acknowledge that slavery as an institution is a moral and political evil in any country.... Their emancipation will sooner result from a mild and melting influence than the storms and contests of fiery controversy. This influence, though slow, is sure. The doctrines and miracles of our Savior have required nearly two thousand years to convert but a small part of the human race, and even among Christian nations what gross errors still exist! While we see the course of the final abolition of slavery is onward, and we give it the aid of our prayers, and all justifiable means in our power, we must leave the progress as well as the result in His hands who sees the end and who chooses to work by slow things,...although the abolitionist must know this, and must see that he has neither the right

nor the power of operating except by moral means and suasion.[37]

To his son, Custis, he writes on December 14, 1860:

> I am not pleased with the course of the 'Cotton States' as they term themselves....One of their plans seems to be the renewal of the slave trade. That I am opposed to on every ground."[38]

And concerning his devotion to preserving the Union, he wrote on January 23, 1861:

> As an American citizen, I take great pride in my country, her prosperity and institutions, and would defend any State if her rights were invaded. But I can anticipate no greater calamity for the country than a dissolution of the Union. It would be an accumulation of all the evils we complain of, and I am willing to sacrifice everything but honor for its preservation.... Secession is nothing but revolution.[39]

Finally, as to the thought of Civil War itself, he writes,

> The country seems to be in a lamentable condition, and may have been plunged into civil war. May God rescue us from the folly of our acts. Save us from selfishness, and teach us to love our neighbors as ourselves.[40]

On April 20, 1861, after refusing to accept command of the Union army in the field, Lee resigned his commission in the army and wrote a series of letters to General Scott and members of his family in which he uses a phrase to emphasize he does not want to fight the North. To his sister in Baltimore, whose husband stayed with the Union, he words it this way: "and save in defense of my native State—with the sincere hope that my poor services may never be needed—I hope I may never be called upon to draw my sword."[41] So for Robert Edward Lee, despite his passionate feelings about the importance of preserving the Union and his disdain for slavery, the honor of doing his duty for his state of Virginia was a value to him that transcended life and one which he would take life or give his life to defend.

For others, it was a passion for their view of liberty and state's rights that caused them to take up arms. In Dabney's preface to his biography of General Jackson, he states:

> The people of the South went to war, because they sincerely believed (what their political fathers had taught them, with one voice, for two generations) that the doctrine of State-sovereignty for which they fought, was absolutely essential as the bulwark of the liberties of the people.[42]

He goes on to devote an entire chapter to a defense of the right and justice of secession, a belief held by General Jackson himself and those seceding states. His defense rests on the following description of what they understood the United States and its Constitution to be.

> Their view of those powers was founded on the following historical facts,...That the former colonies of Great Britain emerged from the Revolutionary War distinct and sovereign political communities or commonwealths, in a word, separate nations, though allied together, and as such were recognized by all the European powers: That, after some years' existence as such, they voluntarily formed a covenant, called the Constitution of the United States, which created a species of government resting upon this compact for its existence and rights; a government which was the creature of the sovereign States, acting as independent nations in forming it: That this compact conferred certain defined powers and duties upon the Central Government, for purposes common to all the States alike, and expressly reserved and prohibited the exercise of all other powers, leaving to the States the management of their own affairs. They, therefore, did not sacrifice their nature as sovereignties, by acceding to the Federal Union; but, by compact, they conceded some of the functions of an independent nation, particularly defined, to the Central Government, retaining all the rest as before.[43]

Although viewing individual states as independent nations may seem a strange concept today, the first state seceded only seventy-three years after the adoption of the US Constitution. Ratification of the proposed Constitution in 1787 wasn't a foregone conclusion. Many states were reluctant to cede power to a central government. One result of the Civil War was it defined America as one nation, but at the time, many good men believed in State first.

And yet for others, the cause was simply one of self-defense. This reason was claimed by both sides, but as the explicit aim of President Lincoln was to bring the seceding states back into the Union by force, many southerners fought to defend their homes and families from an advancing army.

In Edward Everett's Gettysburg speech, he addressed both self-defense and secession in validating the North's prosecution of the war. He stated that "the war is one of self-defense."[44] He discussed South Carolina's attack on Fort Sumter as the first shots of the war and that the Union was forced to respond. (All the while, the South claimed that Lincoln sent eleven ships with 285 guns and 2,400 men to reinforce Sumter on April 8, 1861, to provoke the South at a time when the South still was being led to believe that negotiations would result in the evacuation of Sumter.)[45] Concerning secession, Everett said, "[B]ut it is equally true, that, in adopting the federal Constitution, the States abdicated, by express renunciation, all the most important functions of national sovereignty."[46] His argument was that by ceding to the federal government the power to declare war, raise troops, negotiate treaties, and so on, the individual states joining the Union had given up the powers that distinguished them as separate nations. A state, therefore, once a part of the Union, had no right to secede or claim individual sovereignty.

Of course, what inflamed the debate about state's rights was the issue of slavery. Did the individual states have the right to decide if they would allow slavery, or was it a prerogative of the federal government to prohibit slavery in the states? Ultimately, how that question and the issue of slavery would be decided hinged on the beliefs, policies, and actions of one man, Abraham Lincoln. There are two characteristics that lift Abraham Lincoln above other presidents in American history: foresight and resolve.

Lincoln had the foresight to know that if the ideals of freedom and liberty, upon which the nation was founded, were to continue, it had to be through one united nation. In his June 16, 1858, speech to the convention that would nominate him for Senate candidate, he said, "A house divided against itself cannot stand." Lincoln was an affectionate student of the founders and held many of them in high regard. The proponents of the new Constitution, in 1787, knew they had a difficult task in getting it ratified. The Articles of Confederation, under which the states had been operating, were inadequate in forming a functioning nation exactly because the states were separate sovereigns. There wasn't a binding force upon the states to provide the funding for a national government. The new Constitution proposed to make the citizens of the states citizens of a new nation;

and as citizens of that nation, the national government would have authority over the individual to collect taxes and act for the defense and welfare of the citizens as a nation. This did require a delicate balance between limiting the federal government to the minimum powers necessary to function as a nation and preserving the rights of the states in all other matters. But it was essential that there be one nation.

Alexander Hamilton, James Madison, and to a lesser extent, John Jay published a series of letters in New York newspapers beginning in October of 1787 under the pen name Publius to urge ratification of the new Constitution. They are known as *The Federalist Papers*. The bulk of the first twenty papers address the need for a strong union forming one nation and expose the weaknesses of confederations or the states as independent sovereigns. At the end of "Federalist No. 7," Hamilton writes,

> The probability of incompatible alliances between the different States, or confederacies, and different foreign nations, and the effects of this situation upon the peace of the whole, have been sufficiently unfolded in some preceding papers. From the view they have exhibited, of this part of the subject, this conclusion is to be drawn, that America, if not connected at all, or only by the feeble tie of a simple league offensive and defensive, would by the operation of such opposite and jarring alliances be gradually entangled in all the pernicious labyrinths of European politics and wars; and by the destructive contentions of the parts, into which she was

divided would be likely to become a prey to the artifices and machinations of powers equally the enemies of them all. *Divide et impera* must be the motto of every nation, that either hates, or fears us.[47]

In "Federalist No. 14," Madison states,

> We have seen the necessity of the union as our bulwark against foreign danger, as the conservator of peace among ourselves, as the guardian of our commerce and other common interests, as the only substitute for those military establishments which have subverted the liberties of the old world; and as the proper antidote for the diseases of faction, which have proved fatal to other popular governments, and of which alarming symptoms have been betrayed by our own.[48]

Hamilton explains in "Federalist No. 15,"

> The great and radical vice in the construction of the existing Confederation is in the principle of LEGISLATION for STATES or GOVERNMENTS, in their CORPORATE or COLLECTIVE CAPACITIES and as contradistinguished from the INDIVIDUALS of whom they consist.... The consequence of this is, that though in theory their resolutions concerning those objects are laws, constitutionally binding on the members of the Union, yet in practice they are mere recommendations, which the States observe

or disregard at their option....we must extend the authority of the union to the persons of the citizens, —the only proper objects of government.[49]

It was in this same vein of thought that Lincoln was determined to preserve the Union. An America that was divided into separate nation-states, or separate Confederations, would only bring about the wars and division Hamilton and Madison wrote of. The founders' dream was for a truly new nation based on equality and liberty for all Americans. As for the argument of Dabney in support of secession and the argument of Everett against secession, both were very convincing in their respective positions. But Lincoln based his decisions upon a different premise. In an 1858, letter he wrote, "I believe the declara[tion] that 'all men are created equal' is the great fundamental principle upon which our free institutions rest."[50] Lincoln understood that the ideal of a United States of America was rooted in the Declaration of Independence and that the value of the equality of the individual and the right to "life, liberty, and the pursuit of happiness" could only be preserved and spread through one nation. The Union must be preserved, but the Union also faced an inevitable crisis.

In his "A House Divided" speech, he also made the statement: "In my opinion, it will not cease, until a crisis shall have been reached, and passed."[51] What he was referencing that would not cease was the division and contentions concerning slavery. Lincoln opposed slavery, often making comments that it wasn't right for a man to live off of the labor of another. But he believed it would be a slow process to abolish it. He grew into the position that preserving the Union and emancipation went hand in hand. The Civil War had brought the nation to face the irreconcilable conflict between the Constitution's allowance of slavery and the principles upon which the Constitution was established: the equality of all men, the basis for which rights even exist. The Constitution is the means by which citizens are guaranteed the freedom to exercise their rights, but the foundation for rights is found in the declaration. Lincoln also had the resolve to accept nothing less than preservation and emancipation as an end to the war. And his foresight inspired the nation to bring the Constitution in line with the principles of the declaration through the amendments that were passed after the war.

Some detail has been examined about the Civil War and some of the principal men involved in the war to illustrate the complexities and paradoxes that often are associated with war. On one side was Robert Edward Lee, arguably the most influential man in the South during the war and a man of impeccable character who opposed slavery and secession, but felt his greatest allegiance was to the duty he had to his state of Virginia. On the other side was Abraham Lincoln, the most powerful man in the North and a visionary, who came to the determination that the principles of America's founding could only be carried forward through Union and emancipation. Neither understood the other or wanted war. Lincoln thought Lee "a strange and inexplicable man."[52] Yet neither could stop war from coming. Jackson, Everett, Dabney—the list of names would reach into the hundreds of thousands, truly good men on both sides who held irreconcilable beliefs that they were willing to die for, and it led to an inevitable clash. That is not to deny that there were men who wanted war for their own aggrandizement or slave owners who desired to continue to steal the labor of other men. But the complexities of the Civil War demonstrate that at times, even among good men, war is unavoidable. During the dark late summer days of 1862, before Antietam, Lincoln grappled with these issues and that it all seemed unstoppable, out of everyone's control. He wrote this comment:

> I am almost ready to say this is probably true—that God wills this contest, and wills that it shall not end yet. By his mere quiet power, on the minds of the now contestants, He could have either *saved* or *destroyed* the Union without a human contest. Yet the contest began. And having begun He could give the final victory to either side any day. Yet the contest proceeds.[53]

America needs a war policy that has at its foundation an understanding that at times war is unavoidable. If the Civil War was unavoidable because of the irreconcilable beliefs of good men, how much more is war unavoidable when evil threatens the life and rights of US citizens? An understanding of unavoidability provides a foundation for preparedness, a determination to act quickly when threats arise and are recognized, and the resolve to prosecute wars in a manner that eliminates or destroys the threat.

To develop a successful war policy, a policy that saves American lives, minimizes enemy casualties, and results in victory, both war and victory need to be clearly defined. Is war only defined by violence and aggression? Various civilizations throughout history have made violence and aggression a part of their culture. Sparta in ancient Greece built their society around war and the warrior. The Vikings used looting and pillaging to procure wealth and increase land holdings. Some Native American tribes viewed acts of war and raiding as passages to manhood. Acts of aggression that aren't based on ideological disagreements or defense of home but show a disrespect for the rights of others resemble an act of crime committed on a national or societal level more than an act of warfare. To the victims of such aggression, the end result of loss of life, liberty, and property is the same, and calling it societal crime doesn't bring comfort, but defining war by such aggression isn't helpful to developing a war policy for nations that recognize human rights. There is a distinction between war and criminal acts. Granted, the term "criminal acts" suggests a moral judgment, which is different for each society, often based upon the religious views of a society. And many times, those differences in moral values are the very reason for conflicts. America is fortunate to have an expression of national moral values based on natural rights enshrined in its Declaration of Independence.

Niccolò Machiavelli was a Florentine statesman who, in 1513, wrote a classic book on theories of political power entitled *The Prince*. Often criticized for promoting methods or morals that are frowned upon in western civilization today, Machiavelli's work reveals an adept understanding of human nature. In speaking of his view of legitimate roads to power versus criminal actions, he wrote, "Still, to slaughter fellow-citizens, to betray friends, to be devoid of honour, [sic] pity, and religion, cannot be counted as merits, for these are means which may lead to power, but which confer no glory."[54] Criminal acts do not define legitimate war.

Dictionaries define war as an armed or hostile conflict between nations or states. But a definition of war that helps to develop a policy needs to be more inclusive than a description of the physical destruction of an enemy's resistance. Physical destruction is certainly a part of war, generally the part that comes to mind when the word *war* is mentioned. However, that destruction is not the end objective; it is one means of achieving the objective, victory. Yet what is victory? Defining war as it relates to policy can be accomplished better if victory is defined first.

Victory, as it relates to war, is the submission of one side to the *will* of the other. So victory itself is easy to determine if there is a clear and concise explanation of will, goals, and objectives in a conflict. Returning to the example of the Civil War, President Lincoln's expressed will was simply that the southern states return to the Union, obeying the Constitution and laws passed under its authority, including the newly passed Thirteenth Amendment abolishing slavery. Once the soldiers of the South laid down their arms and swore allegiance to the United States, the conflict ended. *The essential and critical part of any war policy is a clear, realistic expression of the objective of the conflict.* Once that is defined and victory can be measured by that standard, war itself becomes any action that brings about the submission of the opposing side to that objective. Those actions aren't limited to armed conflict and destruction, though that may be necessary to remove resistance, but should include economic and internal political actions, as necessary, to achieve victory.

Carl von Clausewitz served as a Prussian military officer and war college educator and administrator. He fought for Prussia against Napoleon was captured and later released. When Napoleon requested Prussian troops for his campaign against Russia, Clausewitz left Prussia and aided the Russians in repelling Bonaparte. After the Prussians broke from France, Clausewitz again joined the Prussian forces and fought at Waterloo. Over the course of his military career, from 1793 to 1831, he was a keen student of the conduct of war. A prolific writer, he took notes and wrote essays on the topic of war. In 1818, when he assumed the office of the director of the General War College in Berlin, he began in earnest to take his thoughts from these notes and essays and write his eight-book treatise entitled *On War*. Much of the last twelve years of his life were devoted to completing this monumental work.[55] The book is an in-depth discussion of the theory, practice, and science of war. Clausewitz described his work in a preface written around 1818 this way: "Its scientific character consists in an attempt to investigate the essence of the phenomena of war and to indicate the links between these phenomena and the nature of their component parts."[56]

However, Clausewitz realized the many uncontrollable variables of war precluded it from being reduced to a pure science: repeatable results based on observation, hypothesis, and experimentation. Thus he added this description of his treatise: "It would obviously be a mistake to determine the form of an ear of wheat by analyzing the chemical elements of its kernel, since all one needs to do is to go to a wheat field to see the grown ears. Analysis and observation, theory and experience must never disdain or exclude each other; on the contrary, they support each other. The propositions of this book therefore, like short spans of an arch, base their axioms on the secure foundation either of experience or the nature of war as such, and are thus adequately buttressed."[57]

Clausewitz died prematurely on November 16, 1831, possibly from a heart attack, and never completed the book to his complete satisfaction. As late as 1827, he had left notes detailing his plan to revise the entire work. He only considered the first few chapters of book one complete. Despite that, the eight books that make up *On War* remain a timeless description of war and how to successfully conduct it.

Clausewitz made two statements that are pertinent to this discussion of the definition of war and victory. The concept of the first—"War is thus an act of force to compel our enemy to do our will"—has been discussed as it relates to defining victory.[58] The other statement is probably the most often-quoted statement by Clausewitz: "War is not merely an act of policy but a true political instrument, a continuation of political intercourse, carried on with other means."[59] Many times this is paraphrased to "war is the continuation of policy by other means." Those "other means" being referred to are the use of destructive force to eliminate the resistance of an opposing side's submission to the will of the other. Clausewitz recognized and taught that war cannot simply be unleashed destruction but that destruction is always related to a purpose. Without a clearly defined statement of purpose— will, goals, and objectives—combatants may be hurled at each other and lives would be lost without an understanding of why. The military being an instrument of government, that purpose is always political in nature. It therefore behooves political leaders to be serious and resolute in defining purpose realistically. Then all the forces of war—military, economic, and political—can be concentrated on achieving victory, submission to that purpose.

Absent from this discussion of war has been an examination of the question, can wars be just? Some would argue that war and taking human life is never justified. For nations that express a recognition of the sanctity of human life and that life is a natural right, justifying taking human life does seem contradictory. The brutality of war also makes it easy to say it is never right or just. Clausewitz said, "It would be futile—even wrong—to try and shut one's eyes to what war really is from sheer distress at its brutality."[60] Clausewitz made that statement in regard to the recognition that the central element in war is destroying the enemy. His point: it would be wrong to restrain that destruction only on the basis that it is so brutal. Taking human life cannot be anything but brutal. But it would be just as wrong to say that war is *never* justified on the basis of its brutality because that denies a fundamental aspect of the reality of human existence. That reality is, the world is ruled by force. That is not a pleasant thought. That is not something people who desire peace and good will want. But it is a reality that can't be changed, only recognized and responded to.

Evil exists in the world. Evil can be defined as infringing on the natural rights of men: taking away life, liberty, or property. That evil is expressed both by individuals and nations. When a nation motivated by evil desires moves against another nation, brutality occurs. The only way to stop it is to match that brutality through armed conflict and destroy the capability of the aggressor nation to carry out its desires. The human heart, bent on evil, cannot be changed by wishing it so. But it is possible to forcefully take away the ability to physically carry out acts of evil and destroy those determined to perpetrate it. In that paradigm, war is just. And it is the only *peaceful* response to the reality of human existence.

War is a peaceful response to aggression. Imagine a world where evil is not restrained. Society would break down into a daily violent struggle for primitive survival. A peaceful and prosperous society can only be maintained through military strength and crushing threats that would disrupt that peace and prosperity. Two important writings on war and military strategy are attributed to ancient Chinese generals Sun Tzu and Sun Pin. Not much is known in detail about either or if they even actually authored the works that are attributed to them. Some say Sun Pin (Sun Bin) is a descendant of Sun Tzu, and others say that he was an ancestor of Sun Tzu. However, the literature they are credited with dates back 2,500 years and is highly regarded and studied for its wisdom regarding war and leadership. The literature attributed to Sun Tzu is titled *The Art of War* and Sun Pin's, *The Art of Warfare*, although Sun Pin's is occasionally referred to by other names to avoid confusion with Sun Tzu. Both of these works exist today in various English translations. There are two quotes from Sun Pin that are relevant to war not only being just but also necessary to preserve peace. "Victory in war is for the survival of a threatened state, and the protection of its people. Defeat in war means the destruction of property and bondage of the people."[61] The second quote is even more striking in its direct address of the enigma that peace and prosperity can only be maintained by the judicious use of force. "One should desire to increase love, spread righteousness, endow the arts and humanities, wear fine clothing, and put an end to conflict and strife. After all this is what Yao and Shun wanted, but even they could not attain it without the use of the military to ensure peace."[62]

War is also justifiable within the context of the role of government. In today's political climate, many people assume government's role is to provide education and philanthropy to its citizens. But in actuality, government's reason for existing is to secure the rights of men. The US Declaration of Independence states, "That to secure these rights, Governments are instituted among Men, deriving their just powers from the consent of the governed." Among, but not limited to, those rights referred to are the natural rights of life, liberty, and the pursuit of happiness. What the declaration calls the "pursuit of Happiness" has been termed by other writers on natural rights as the right to own property. Frédéric Bastiat, a French economist and statesman, termed some of these same concepts as "life, faculties, and production."[63] The essence of both of these statements is that all humanity has a right to live free, to use their gifts and talents, and to produce goods and services with property for their enjoyment and sustenance in life. Security conveys the meaning of being safe, unthreatened, and protected. So the true role of government is to provide the security necessary for people to live and enjoy these rights. That security is provided internally through laws that allow businesses free opportunity to compete and protect citizens from criminal activity. Externally, that security is provided through the military defending the country from any group or nation that would take away the life, freedom, or property of its citizens. Within that context, war is just and necessary and a requirement of government. "For that war is just which is necessary, and those arms are sacred from which we derive our only hope."[64]

The preceding discourse on the nature of war, its unavoidability, and justness demand that a central question be answered: how should war be prosecuted? It was stated earlier that a successful war policy should save American lives, minimize enemy casualties, and result in victory. Casualties of war are not statistics; they are husbands and wives, sons and daughters, brothers and sisters, fathers and mothers. Every life is precious. Even though the role of government and nature of the world demand that wars be fought to secure rights, it is incumbent upon government to prosecute wars in a way that values the life and sacrifice of its soldiers. American soldiers, their families, and the citizens who support them deserve to know that what they are doing matters. They deserve to know why they are asked to risk their lives and what the objective of the war is. They deserve to know their sacrifice is not in vain.

2

Saving Lives

A policy for prosecuting war has many facets. Of course, the most obvious is an effective fighting force capable of destroying enemy resistance. America has the best fighting force in the world that if properly supplied and supported is capable of destroying any opposing force. Since World War II, the problems that have occurred with America's war policy have fallen within the political realm. That isn't surprising given Clausewitz's axiom, "War is…a true political instrument, a continuation of political intercourse, carried on with other means." It is this aspect of war that needs to be addressed. A foundation needs to be laid for a successful war policy that is based on the reality of war and human nature that can support public understanding and shape public opinion, which in turn can forge the political will necessary to ensure victory. Public opinion and political will are the elements that give direction and purpose to America's military. So this is not a discussion of tactics and strategy, of which Clausewitz said, "Tactics teaches the use of armed forces in the engagement; strategy, the use of engagements for the object of the war."[65] Those discussions are for the generals. Rather, this is a discussion aimed at the "heart and temper" of the nation. For: "All these cases have shown what an *enormous contribution the heart and temper of a nation* [italics mine] can make to the sum total of its politics, war potential, and fighting strength."[66]

There are six foundational elements by which public opinion and political will can be solidified into a launchpad for military victory:

- Be prepared.
- Act before a crisis.
- Clearly define realistic objectives.
- Act decisively.
- Prosecute war aggressively.
- Persevere.

Be Prepared

War will happen. It is unavoidable. History demonstrates that it is not a matter of if war will occur, but only when. It would be nice if that were not the case, but decisions cannot be based on wishes. Prudence requires decisions to be made on the best understanding of ascertained facts. Accepting the unavoidability of war recognizes the need to be prepared for it. Some time was spent examining the causes of the American Civil War and the motivations of some of those involved in that conflict to show that wars can occur because of a clash of values that each side regards more sacred than life. In Clausewitz's vast experience on different battlefields, he recognized that "there are usually no hostile feelings between individuals."[67] So even though there may not be hostile feelings between parties, war can still break out when neither side will back away from their value-based position. That is one cause of the unavoidability of war. How much more is war unavoidable when there is genuine hatred by one party against another? That is clearly evident by the actions of extremist Muslim terrorists in their war against western civilization. It is a war on their part fueled by hatred. That hatred cannot be reasoned with, and the war is unavoidable. This unavoidability must be met with preparedness.

Despite the fact that it is easy to see that war will happen, most nations find themselves unprepared when attacked. At the start of both world wars, the United States was woefully unprepared even though the wars had been raging in Europe. Ten years before Japan attacked Pearl Harbor, it had started its aggressive expansion into parts of China in 1931. It wasn't until May of 1940 that Roosevelt began asking in earnest for increases to the defense budget and expanded war production.[68] Delays in preparedness cost lives. Wars are lengthened by the time involved in increasing troop strength and armament, and troops in the field at the outset of a conflict are understrength, which leaves them fighting at a disadvantage and susceptible to higher casualties. It is irresponsible for a nation to be unprepared for war and an injustice to its enlisted troops when they aren't fully equipped and supported.

There is a side to human nature that wants to avoid conflict. That is good and something that should be recognized and used as a factor in developing a deterrent strategy. The degree to which a nation wants to avoid a conflict is directly proportional to the consequences of the conflict. A nuclear deterrent strategy has proven very effective in avoiding a nuclear war with the nations that have acquired these weapons to date because the consequences of a nuclear war are greater than any perceived benefit from a war. But the desire to avoid conflict can't be used as an excuse to avoid preparing for war. There is a mistaken view that all that is needed for peace is for one side to lay down their weapons and say they will not fight. That will only lead to subjugation and is a denial of the reality of human existence. The world stage can be likened to a playground. The bully always picks on the ones who can't or won't hit back. The surest way to stay safe is to present an image of strength and ability to defend oneself.

The vigilance, expense, and effort required to stay in a constant state of preparedness is wearisome. During times of peace, people often begin to question if it is worth it and are lulled into a false sense of security. And if people misunderstand the role of government—to secure rights—

defense spending is questioned and often cut. But all other expenditures are secondary in importance to defense. Without a strong national defense that secures the liberty of citizens, other programs and spending become irrelevant when that nation is swallowed up by an aggressor. Machiavelli's instructions are still relevant by application today when he said, "A prince, therefore, should have no care or thought but for war, and for the regulations and training it requires, and should apply himself exclusively to this as his peculiar province; for war is the sole art looked for in one who rules." He also said, "A prince, therefore, ought never to allow his attention to be diverted from warlike pursuits, and should occupy himself with them even more in peace than in war."[69] It is a government's primary duty to be in a constant state of preparedness for war.

Communism and capitalism are opposing ideologies. Yet during the Second World War, the communist Soviet Union joined forces with the Allies fighting the Axis powers of Germany, Italy, and Japan. For a short while, the old adage "The enemy of my enemy is my friend" came into play. With the defeat of the Axis powers, a new era of war was introduced between the Soviet Union and the United States. That war became known as the Cold War. It was termed *cold* because open combat, the usual central element of war, was avoided for fear of an escalation into a nuclear holocaust. The struggle between communism and capitalism did erupt into actual fighting wars around the globe, most notable for the United

States in Korea and Vietnam. But the Cold War continued alongside these "hot" wars. It wasn't until the last half of the 1980s that it started to wind down with talks between President Reagan and Soviet's general secretary Mikhail Gorbachev and ended, at least with the Soviet Union, when that union was dissolved on December 25, 1991.

The Cold War provides a fitting example of the benefit of military preparedness. Toward the end of the 1970s, during the Carter administration, defense spending had been cut, and America's military had lost respect in the eyes of the world with the failure of the Iranian hostage rescue in April 1980. That mission, named Eagle Claw, resulted in the death of eight American servicemen, the loss of several helicopters, and a C-130 aircraft—all without even making contact with the enemy. In December of 1979, the Soviet Union had moved into Afghanistan and established a puppet government. Absent a clear, strong foreign policy with a well-funded and prepared military to back it up, the aggressors of the world were free to inflict their will without fear of retaliation from the United States. Unpreparedness invites conflict.

The election of Ronald Reagan in 1980 brought a change in policy to Washington. Building up the military became a top priority. Communism was labeled what it truly is, evil, and foreign policy was based on stopping its spread. Among Reagan's military programs was the Strategic Defense Initiative (SDI), also known as Star Wars. It was given that name because the concept was a space-based weapons system that would be able to destroy any incoming nuclear missiles before they were able to reach the United States. Reagan's policies were effectively concentrating military, economic, and political forces against the Soviet Union to stop communist aggression, and it worked. Decades of communism had taken its toll on Soviet production. Internally, the economy was in shambles. Money wasn't available to attempt to keep up with advances in American military technology and armament output. In September of 1986, Soviet foreign minister Eduard Shevardnadze delivered a letter to President Reagan that Gorbachev was ready to negotiate, and by May of 1987, "the Soviets announced a formal military doctrine—one aimed simply at defending their homeland."[70] The determination to build up America's military and be prepared for conflict had won the Cold War without an armed conflict. Preparedness saves lives.

A fascinating side to the Cold War is illustrative of how preparedness is a strong deterrent that can avert war and keep a country strong in the midst of global threats. That side is the story of the submarine service. The development and construction of Soviet nuclear-powered submarines that could remain submerged under the ocean for months at a time and were capable of launching ballistic missiles posed a serious threat to United States national security. Both fixed and mobile land-based missiles could be located by satellite, spy plane, or spies and land intelligence. These in turn could be targeted and watched for indications of being prepared to launch, so the United States wouldn't be caught off guard and the Soviets would know a retaliatory strike would be immediately launched by the United States. But ballistic missiles launched from submarines in unknown locations created the possibility of those missiles taking out America's capability to respond. Deterrent as prevention for a nuclear war depends on the image, backed up by evidence, of a no-win situation. America's committed use of research and technology created submarines that stayed ahead of the Soviet subs. American SSNs (nuclear-powered attack submarines) were able to keep track of Soviet submarine activity. They followed enemy subs and stayed in position to destroy them in the event a launch was detected. It was soon discovered how valuable the submarine could be to gathering intelligence in general. As enemy subs were followed around the ocean for miles upon miles, the data that was collected helped to form a picture of Soviet tactics and plans. Many men gave their lives in this silent underwater cold war through accidents and dangerous missions that went wrong.

One of the most daring missions happened in November of 1971. The *Halibut* had been used briefly in the early 1960s to carry missiles, but it was an oddly designed submarine with a very large hatch, and it was quickly replaced with the newer *Polaris* subs. It was refitted in 1965 as a research vessel, but in 1971, it received a new mission. Stretched across the floor of the Okhotsk sea was a telephone cable that connected the Soviet submarine base near Petropavlovsk on the Kamchatka peninsula to the Soviet mainland. The Okhotsk sea and Kamchatka Peninsula are located northeast of Japan and west of the Aleutian Islands. In 1971, it was just a theory that the cable even existed; and if it did, no one knew where it was located in the sea. The foresight of a man named James Bradley and his determination to attempt to find and tap the cable are a prodigious example of American commitment to the defense of this nation. In November 1971, the courageous crew of the *Halibut* traveled inside Soviet waters and found the cable. Divers attached an inductive tap to it and began listening to the conversations of the Soviet Navy. The success of this mission led to the establishment of a program of specially fitted submarines to conduct cable-tapping missions, which provided an enormous wealth of valuable life-saving intelligence. That intelligence was gathered with great risk by crews that possessed exceptional bravery. Cable-tapping subs were equipped with self-destructing demolitions. If something went wrong, the sub would be scuttled, the mission denied, and grieving families would be left not knowing what really happened to their loved ones.[71]

Such courage and determination exemplify the effort needed to be fully prepared for war. The actions of the entire submarine service during the Cold War played a vital role in keeping America safe and thwarting the aggression of the Soviet Union. Sherry Sontag and Christopher Drew make this comment in their excellent book, *Blind Man's Bluff*, on the subject. "The Soviet Union's efforts to keep up with the

United States military, especially its efforts to create a force of missile subs that could evade US attack subs during the opening salvos of a nuclear war, clearly contributed to the country's ultimate bankruptcy."[72]

The submarine fleet has clearly demonstrated its value to the security of the United States. But the question remains if America still has the determination to maintain that level of preparedness. In the late 1980s, the number of America's attack submarines reached a high of ninety-eight, and the high number for missile subs was forty-one.[73] In 2014, the number of attack subs had dwindled to fifty-five with about forty of those being Los Angeles–class subs from the late 1970s and 1980s, which were in need of retirement. By 2028, the attack sub fleet is estimated to be only forty-one. The fourteen remaining ballistic missile subs will be obsolete in the 2020s.[74] There is an order out for ten more of the new Virginia-class submarines, but that won't keep pace with the loss of older subs being retired. With China's aggressive naval expansion, the need for the submarine's quiet ability to gather intelligence and watch the actions of other nations remains great.

The submarine fleet has been looked at as just one example of the need to be prepared militarily. But all aspects of armed forces need to be equally prepared. Often, the big projects get attention and funding while the smaller elements may be overlooked. Adequate ammunition stock needs to be maintained for troops to train. Parts need to be available to keep equipment running and operational. Divisions need to be kept combat-ready; that requires constant supply and upkeep, not neglect. Numbers of planes, troops, and vessels can and should vary with situations, potential threats, and historical evidence. But those decisions need to be based on a realistic interpretation of world events and not a wishful belief that the military isn't necessary. And whatever the overall size of the military is, it needs to be fully trained, prepared, and equipped to be used.

There is one more important aspect of preparedness that is crucial. The capability to design and produce weapons and armament must always be kept in place and ready to be ramped up into high production. If at times it is practical to reduce the number of ships, planes, tanks, and so on, the ability to produce them quickly is vital in any conflict and to respond to changing situations. A comment in an article discussing the recent order for the ten new submarines illustrates the point well: "However attractive the notion of spacing construction out may appear from a budgetary perspective, it creates significant long-term problems with the infrastructure and human capital of the shipbuilding industry. Of the major nuclear submarine operators, only China appears to have developed the capability of maintaining long-term, nearly continuous production, as Russian efforts to jumpstart the industry continue to meet with difficulties."[75] During a conflict, time can't be wasted building the factories and training the skilled workers necessary to produce high-tech equipment. Production and technical skill levels of military hardware output need to be included in preparedness plans.

Preparedness is an essential element in a successful war policy and vital to saving American lives. The better prepared a nation is for war, the less likely it will be in a war. The deterrent effect of a strong military, and the resolve displayed to use it to defend American values, crosses all cultural lines and is a universal language that everyone understands. But deterrent hinges on preparedness.

Act before a Crisis

"The Romans, therefore, foreseeing evils while they were yet far off, always provided against them, and never suffered them to take their course for the sake of avoiding war; since they knew that war is not so to be avoided, but is only postponed to the advantage of the other side.…nor did the maxim *leave it to Time*, [sic]…ever recommend itself to them."[76]

Machiavelli's reference to the wisdom of the Romans in taking care of problems before they became a bigger problem is still relevant today. It is essential for a nation to take action before events become a crisis. Postponing the inevitable only allows the enemy to become better prepared, which in turn leads to a greater conflict and greater loss of life.

There are two tragic dates in American history that poignantly illustrate the devastation that can come from waiting and hoping for a peace that's not possible: December

7, 1941, and September 11, 2001. On each of these days, over two thousand Americans died.

In July of 1940, when America restricted the export of oil and other raw materials to select nations, Japan was on the restricted list. Badly needed fuel stocks for Japan's long war in China began to dwindle. From that point, Japan turned its attention to the South Pacific, and war with the United States became inevitable. The attack on Pearl Harbor was a preemptive strike by the Japanese to keep the United States from interfering with Japan's conquest of the region. Japan believed the United States wouldn't stand down as they moved on the East Indies. It was a hope, by the United States, against all the evidence of Japanese actions, that peace could still be maintained and that false hope cost the lives of over two thousand at Pearl Harbor. Islamic terrorists had given equally long indications of their declaration of war against the United States as the Japanese had sixty years earlier when they flew hijacked planes into the Twin Towers. From the bombing of the USS *Cole* in 2000, back to the first attempt to bring down the World Trade Center in 1993, the intentions of the enemy were not hidden. Yet because no action was taken against them, over 2,700 people died on 9/11. Acting before a crisis saves lives.

The natural tendency for peaceable people is to want to avoid conflict. For that reason, hope is held onto longer than is prudent in many cases. But government, charged with securing the rights of its citizens, doesn't have the luxury of hoping beyond what the evidence suggests. The maxim "Actions speak louder than words" isn't just applicable to personal relationships. It is an imperative truth to be observed in diplomatic relations. In dealing with other nations or groups the motto is "Believe what they do, be skeptical of what they say."

Does a preemptive strike define that nation as the aggressor? Not if the strike is a response to definite intentions of hostility. The American government should act as a watchful eagle, ready to pounce on any threat to national security. The aggressors are the groups or nations that, through their actions and words, declare their intent to harm America and are only waiting on the time or means to fulfill their desire. In that case, it is wrong to wait for an attack or to wait until the enemy has the means to carry out an attack before taking action against them. The safest course of action is to destroy threats when they are still a thought rather than waiting until they mature into a capable reality.

Perhaps the greatest example of a failure to act before a crisis came before the onset of the war in Europe in World War II. Neville Chamberlain is the poster child for political weakness and appeasement, made so by his infamous "peace for our time" speech after signing the Munich Agreement on September 30, 1938. But in fairness to him, he was only the prominent face representing weak and irresolute governments that had no interest in making a stand. Adolf Hitler had revealed to the world his political ideology and plans in *Mein Kampf*. After years of political maneuvering, he became chancellor of Germany in 1933. He immediately began to act to bring to pass his dreams. In October 1933, Germany pulls out of the League of Nations and begins to openly build their military in violation of the Versailles treaty. Hitler announces another violation of the treaty in 1935 when he reveals the existence of the German air force. In March 1936, German troops march into the Rhineland, demilitarized by the Versailles treaty, with only protests from France and Britain. Hitler made this move against the advice of his generals who warned him that the military was not ready for a confrontation should France respond with force. A prime opportunity to crush the German military before it became a strong efficient machine escaped. All this took place before Chamberlain took office as prime minister of Britain in May 1937. Chamberlain simply continued the same policy of France and Britain to ignore Hitler and hope he would be content with his own little realm, but he continued to demonstrate his ambition in the coming years. Austria was annexed by Germany in March 1938, and Hitler next turned toward Czechoslovakia.

The Munich Agreement in September 1938 occurred over Hitler's intention to join the Sudetenland to Germany. This was a territory in Czechoslovakia next to the German border in which many German-speaking people lived. In Munich, Chamberlain went beyond the conciliation of France and his own government when he offered up part of Czechoslovakia to Hitler, acting without the knowledge of the French or support of some in his own cabinet. This was a fatal mistake by Chamberlain. Before his intervention, Czechoslovakian president Benes was determined to defend the integrity of his country. Part of the Czech army had been mobilized the preceding May. The Czech army was slightly smaller than Germany's but was well trained and equipped. The French, although less prepared for war and not enthusiastic, seemed resigned to aid Czechoslovakia, and the Germans would have only been able to put up light resistance on their western front to be fully engaged in the east against the Czechs. With British help, there was a good chance through war to stop Hitler then. Chamberlain's intervention destroyed that possibility. Able to convince his own government to support his plan, he gave the timid French a way out of their commitment to Czechoslovakia and signed his worthless paper pledging Germany and Britain to *talk* out their differences. Czechoslovakia, abandoned and sold out by her allies, capitulated to Hitler.[77]

No one knows what the outcome would have been if Chamberlain had let France and Britain come to Czechoslovakia's aid. Both France and Britain had wasted the preceding years' opportunity to strengthen their militaries and be prepared for war. But even in the next year before war actually did break out, September 1, 1939, Germany far outpaced Britain and France in arms production and troop strength. Certainly, the outcome of going to war with

Germany in 1938 could not have been worse than waiting a year, and possibly, millions of lives may have been spared by an early intervention. But even looking at the years prior to 1938, it is sad that events were allowed to reach the point they eventually did. Opportunities for acting before a crisis were missed, and lives were lost.

The year 2015 began with a continued crisis in waiting that is being ignored on a real level. A show is ongoing that pretends serious effort is being put into finding a solution, but the reality is the United States is being played by an enemy. That enemy is the hardline Iranian government and its uranium enrichment program for the purpose of developing nuclear weapons. It is extremely unfortunate that this problem has been allowed to continue for so long without being seriously addressed. Unfortunate for the Iranian people. Of all the nations in the Middle East, Iran is one of the nations with the greatest potential to be a thriving economic bastion of democratic liberty. It has a rich history, strong educational foundations, and a young demographic that is hungry for true democracy and freedom. The desire of the United States should always be for people to live in freedom and have the liberty to develop the great potential that lies within each individual. The United States can aid that happening, but freedom is something that the people of a nation must take up for themselves and embrace.

Currently, Iran is producing enriched uranium in violation of the UN Security Council, which ordered production to be suspended. Iran has no commercial purpose for enriching uranium and tried to conceal that it was being produced. There is an above-and-below ground facility at Natanz where this is taking place.[78] The only purpose Iran has for enriched uranium is for use in weapons. Some think it is hypocritical for the United States to tell Iran it can't have nuclear weapons when the US has so many of its own. The United States has used its nuclear arsenal to preserve peace in the world and save lives. The United States government is based on morally superior values that recognize the equality of all men and the right to life, liberty, and property. The current Iranian government recognizes no such rights for all humanity and has been a state sponsor of terrorism. A nuclear-armed Iran threatens the security of the United States, Israel, and the world.

The current government of Iran has given ample evidence of its hostile intentions. Mahmoud Ahmadinejad was elected president of Iran in 2005. (Elections are not free and fair. Only candidates approved by the Guardian Council may even run.) Throughout his eight-year presidency, he made numerous outrageous comments denying the World War II Jewish holocaust and stating, "Israel should be wiped off the map."[79] Iran's current president, Hassan Rouhani, talks more moderately and expresses his desire to improve relations with the United States, but it's unclear if that is his real personal belief or if he is just a token voice to fool the world that the Iranian government wants to negotiate on uranium enrichment. The actions of the government haven't changed since Ahmadinejad has left office. The highest position of power in the country is the held by the supreme leader Ayatollah Ali Khamenei. Parliament is controlled by hardliners who enable the government to continue its support of terrorism, suppress freedom, and commit human rights abuses.

Here are a few examples of what takes place inside Iran. Citizens are officially banned from using Facebook, Twitter, and YouTube, and the government is actively working to control Internet access. Journalists are arrested, imprisoned, or detained for unfavorable reporting of the regime. In May 2014, six young adult Iranians were given a suspended sentence of six months in prison and ninety-one lashes for making a dance video to Pharrell Williams's song "Happy," which went viral on Youtube. A woman was executed in 2014 for killing a man who was sexually assaulting her. Religious expression is restricted, Christians are persecuted, and prisoners are often tortured. A government such as this cannot be allowed to possess nuclear weapons.

Perhaps the greatest display of the true colors of the Iranian leadership were revealed after the 2009 elections. Mahmoud Ahmadinejad was reelected, by questionable results, in a surprise contest with Mir-Hossein Mousavi. Mousavi was a former prime minister of Iran in the 1980s. He was allowed to run in the election as a token opposition candidate because his long absence from politics made it unlikely he would gain any support. But Mousavi's reform platform unleashed the pent-up frustrations of the populace, and he had wide support in the election. Anger over allegations of election fraud fueled protests that started on June 13, 2009. For the next six months, protests against the election process, regime, and supreme leader occurred. And each time they were met with brutal force. "Thousands of protesters were beaten, hundreds were arrested and dozens were killed by snipers."[80]

Despite all this evidence to the contrary, Iran is treated by the nations involved in the talks about uranium enrichment—United States, the United Kingdom, France, Germany, Russia, and China—as if they legitimately desire a solution. Based on what Iran is doing, and not what they say, Iran's current regime has no intention of stopping uranium enrichment and is continuing other programs that indicate a plan to develop a nuclear weapon. Deadlines for talks come and go; the UN paper tiger waves its demands in the air while the Iranians smile, stall, and keep enriching uranium. It's time to act now, before a crisis, and possibly save hundreds of thousands, or millions, of lives.

Clearly Define Realistic Objectives

"No one starts a war—or rather, no one in his senses ought to do so—without first being clear in his mind what he intends to achieve by that war and how he intends to conduct it" (Carl Von Clausewitz).[81]

Earlier, in defining war and victory, this statement was made: "The essential and critical part of any war policy is a clear, realistic expression of the objective of the conflict." Why that is critical was discussed too. The best prepared and equipped military in the world, no matter how good it is at destroying enemy troops, equipment, and occupying ground, may not contribute to the submission of the opposing side if it isn't destroying those things that bring the will of the enemy into submission. Of the six elements that are a necessary foundation for public opinion and political will to translate into a successful war policy, having clearly defined, realistic objectives has been the greatest failure of the United States. *Realistic* is a key word to focus on. Some time will be spent later looking at specific examples from the past sixty-five years where certain of these elements have been ignored and how that has contributed to uncertainty over the purpose and results of the wars America has been involved in. But for now, the discussion will be limited to understanding what a clearly defined, realistic objective is.

An objective is not something that a nation would *like* to see happen. In 1991, pictures of sick, starving Somali citizens touched the hearts of people around the world. Cries went out for humanitarian aid to be sent to them. But as relief organizations set up operations, the civil war and strife that initially caused the food shortages prevented supplies from reaching those in need. Many of the shipments were taken by various warlords and used for their own profit.

UN resolutions and peacekeepers all failed to provide the security needed to see that food was distributed impartially. Finally, the United States was drawn in, through the desire to see that the suffering ended, to sending troops to secure supply distribution.

The reality that was not addressed was that no long-term solution to the starvation and suffering was possible without a strong central Somalia government to provide basic security for its citizens. That was a completely different objective than guarding food shipments. It would require a different military presence—if some plan could even be conceived to bring about a strong government amid all the warring criminal factions. Eventually the US forces that were in Somalia were drawn into ill-equipped police actions prompted by half-hearted political motivations. Brigadier General John S. Brown, in his introduction to the United States Army's after-action report on Somalia, said, "Greeted initially by Somalis happy to be saved from starvation, US troops were slowly drawn into inter-clan power struggles and ill-defined 'nation-building' missions." The lack of a clearly defined, realistic objective cost American lives. Dr. Richard Stewart's historical overview of the action gave this dim summary.

> Americans consider themselves to be a compassionate people, and the United States Army has a long tradition of humanitarian relief operations both within and outside the continental United States. Never has this humanitarian impulse proven more

> dangerous to follow than in 1992 when the United States intervened to arrest famine in the midst of an ongoing civil war in the east African country of Somalia. Ultimately hundreds of thousands were saved from starvation, but unintended involvement in Somali civil strife cost the lives of thirty American soldiers, four marines, and eight Air Force personnel and created the impression of chaos and disaster.[82]

If the "will" that defined victory was simply to secure food shipments, that was a realistic, achievable goal, as long as it was understood it would be an indefinite commitment. When, during the course of the US involvement in Somalia, the mission changed to some unknown intervention into the Somali Civil War, unrealistic expectations were forced upon the troops there, and lives were lost. As a result of those casualties and the lack of a clearly defined, realistic objective for the US presence in Somalia that the American people could get behind, troops were soon withdrawn from Somalia. That, in turn, left an impression of American weakness and lack of resolve in the eyes of the world, which had dangerous consequences for America on 9/11, as terrorists were emboldened by the perception of a weak nation. None of this is a reflection on the troops who served and fought valiantly in Somalia. On the fateful day that so many lives were lost in events that inspired the movie *Black Hawk Down*, US troops completed their mission. They were simply outnumbered and lacked the equipment required to safely perform it. Those are the consequences of political ignorance of the need for clearly defined, realistic objectives.

It is always best to define the will by which victory can be measured, in the narrowest terms possible. That makes it easier to understand the objective and purpose of the war and allows the forces of war (military, economic, and political) to be concentrated on the objective. Referring back to the previously discussed uranium enrichment project of the Iranians, what would a realistic objective look like? First, wars that are intended to "overthrow the enemy—to render him politically helpless or militarily impotent, thus forcing him to sign whatever peace we please" are long, costly, difficult, and depend on breaking the will of the enemy to succeed.[83] The experience of the United States in Iraq and Afghanistan attribute to this fact. Wars of that nature should be a last resort based on egregious circumstances. Second, the nature, character, and culture of the enemy must always be taken into account in realistically assessing the possibilities of what can be accomplished. In the case of the Iranians, it has already been mentioned that there is a large young demographic group that has put themselves at great risk and sacrifice to demonstrate their desire for free elections and better human rights. It's important for the United States not to alienate this group any more than it has already alienated them by failing to publicly support the demonstrations for change that occurred in 2009. America's first interest for the people of any nation should be for their freedom and liberty. America cannot give that to people, but they can take up freedom for themselves, and they should always know the United States supports them. At this point, what is the primary national security concern with Iran? The development of nuclear weapons. A realistic, defined objective would simply be to make sure they do not develop them. Militarily, that may involve destroying the capability to produce them at Natanz if that is feasible. Economic and political forces can be used as well, but they must be aggressive to accomplish the goal. Halfhearted measures in war, economic and political as well, are dangerous because they give the impression of weakness and lack of resolve. Machiavelli observed of human nature that "a Prince [nation] is despised when he is seen to be fickle, frivolous, effeminate, pusillanimous, or irresolute, against which defects he ought therefore most carefully to guard, striving so to bear himself that greatness, courage, wisdom, and strength may appear in all his actions."[84]

The United States also needs a clearly defined, realistic objective in regard to the war on terror. The war on terror is unique in that it is not a war against a nation with defined borders but against groups of differing hierarchy that exist and move among different nations. The attempt to solve the problem of terrorism by regime change and nation-building in Iraq and Afghanistan has proven unsuccessful. Iraq has been lost as a free democratic nation by the early withdrawal of US forces and failure to understand the dynamics of the culture.

One of those dynamics is the often violent clash between the Shiite and Sunni sects of Islam. Those clashes date back to disagreements over the Prophet Muhammad's successor. Shiites believe that Muhammad's authority was passed to his son-in-law Ali. While Sunnis believe that Muhammad did not appoint a successor, and they recognize the authority of the first caliphs. The two sects have had long violent wars that date back centuries. Some of the most notable are the conflicts between the Ottoman Empire and the Safavid Empire. Geographically, the Ottoman Empire was located in modern-day Turkey; and the Safavid Empire, in Persia, today known as Iran. The country of Iraq is located between Turkey and Iran and has a mixed Sunni and Shiite population. The sectarian violence that has and does plague Iraq is rooted in this ancient conflict. As long as the United States remained in Iraq to provide security for the country, the various sects were able to begin working together because they had the assurance that they would be protected by the US military. At a minimum, the United States would have had to stay in Iraq and provide that security long enough for a whole generation to grow up seeing cooperation and allowing an environment of trust to be built. But with the early withdrawal of US forces from Iraq, old hatreds and distrusts quickly erupted to the disintegration of the country.

Ali Khedery is a US official who spent many years in Iraq, and much of that personally involved with the former prime minister Nouri al-Maliki. In an article he wrote in

The Washington Post dated July 3, 2014, Khedery described the inability of al-Maliki to work past those longstanding distrusts. Of al-Maliki, he said, "Prone to conspiracy theories after decades of being hunted by Hussein's intelligence services, he was convinced that his Shiite Islamist rival Moqtada al-Sadr was seeking to undermine him."[85]

With the US withdrawal from Iraq, Khedery chronicles al-Maliki's actions this way. "With the Obama administration vowing to end Bush's 'dumb war,' and the continued distraction of the global economic crisis, Maliki seized an opportunity. He began a systematic campaign to destroy the Iraqi state and replace it with his private office and his political party. He sacked professional generals and replaced them with those personally loyal to him. He coerced Iraq's chief justice to bar some of his rivals from participating in the elections in March 2010. After the results were announced and Maliki lost to a moderate, pro-Western coalition encompassing all of Iraq's major ethno-sectarian groups, the judge issued a ruling that awarded Maliki the first chance to form a government, ushering in more tensions and violence."[86]

It was a completely unrealistic goal to believe that a peaceful, free, democratic Iraq could be established and be self-perpetuating in so short a time as the United States was willing to commit to the effort. Now with Iraq splintered and partially occupied by bloodthirsty IS militants, many Americans wonder what the expenditure of American lives purchased in Iraq. Despite the tremendous difficulties, the battle had been won. Security was established, and an embryo of cooperation was forming. But an unrealistic objective that it could continue without a US presence allowed a hard-fought military victory to slip away.

Afghanistan still remains an open book. Afghanistan is a predominately Sunni nation, but lacks a history of unity and a strong central government. Warring tribes and factions have often controlled their own territory within the country. The Taliban still remains a threat to many parts of the nation. Notwithstanding the progress of the Afghan army and the excellent job the US military did in training them, it remains to be seen if the Afghan people can unify together and maintain control of the country without a strong US presence. It appears an overeager withdrawal will leave Afghanistan in the same difficult situation as Iraq.

Given the extreme difficulties of nation-building in the Middle Eastern culture, what is a clear, realistic objective for the war on terror? Even if the United States possessed the public and political will to invest the human resources and time to establish free, democratic states in the area, the financial resources necessary for such an action would make it unfeasible. The enemy, militant Islamic terrorists, disregard all human life (even their own), are fueled by hatred, and do not have any foundation upon which to negotiate. Their goal is a world caliphate, and they will accept nothing less. There is no reasoning with them or reforming them. The only way to respond to such an enemy is at the most basic level of human nature: fear. The actual terrorists need to be hunted and destroyed. Those who harbor and aid them are guilty accomplices and need to know they put their own lives in jeopardy by aiding terrorists. Nations who sponsor terrorism need to feel the consequences of their actions through tough economic sanctions and limited military retaliation when necessary. While the United States carries out that action with one hand, it needs to be made clear that the other hand is extended in peace. The objective of the war on terror should be limited to living free from the threat of terrorism. No policy can change human hearts bent on hatred. The objective of this war should not be to change nations or cultures; it should only be to prevent terror attacks. Those nations and groups inside nations that work to aid in preventing terrorism need to be shown the utmost kindness and US assistance as they work for peace within their own region. But terrorists, their networks, and those who support them need to be dealt extreme prejudice. That is not an easy thing to write, read, or believe, but it is the reality of the world.

A clear realistic objective defines the political will of a war. It is the basis for public support. It gives the military direction, purpose, and scope. It is the most crucial thing a government can do to save lives on both sides of a conflict, and without it, success cannot be measured. Without it, all the other elements that comprise a successful war policy are like pieces from different puzzles thrown in the same box; they won't fit together so it can be seen what was or will be accomplished. "If you cannot see an end to the conflict, then do not attack. You have not worked properly to set the stage for victory" (Sun Tzu).[87]

Act Decisively

There is a military principle that Clausewitz termed: "concentration of forces in space." The meaning is straightforward: keep all military assets positioned so they can be used decisively in the right place at the right time. In explaining this principle, Clausewitz said, "The best strategy is always *to be very strong*; first in general, and then at the decisive point."[88] So how does this military principle fit into a discussion on the elements of understanding necessary to have a strong foundation of public opinion and political will for a successful war policy? It fits, since often the failure to act decisively is because of a fear of public outcry and concern with political correctness. Once a well-defined, realistic objective has been determined, to act decisively is simply to concentrate and use, with vehemence, all military, economic, and political forces necessary to accomplish the objective. To use force in such a way is usually met with shock and criticism from media and then public opinion, which in turn brings a parade of politicians demanding less force be used or that war be prosecuted with less zeal. And in the end, it is the soldiers on the line whose lives are lost and their missions that are compromised because the necessary force wasn't used to accomplish the goal. Another quote from Clausewitz superbly and plainly makes the point.

> Kind-hearted people might of course think there was some ingenious way to disarm or defeat an enemy without too much bloodshed, and might imagine this is the true goal of the art of war. Pleasant as it sounds, it is a fallacy that must be exposed: war is such a dangerous business that the mistakes which come from kindness are the very worst. The maximum use of force is in no way incompatible with the simultaneous use of the intellect.[89]

Wars are horrible, brutal, and bloody, but they happen. There is nothing kind or nice about war. The best course of action in war is to act decisively to end it as soon as possible. Anything less increases the inhumanity of war because more lives are lost on both sides by a weak effort that prolongs and encourages more conflict. If you don't swing to kill the wasp, you just get stung.

Decisive action shortens war. Time can be an enemy in many different areas of life. It is an enemy to the physical body, an enemy to deadlines that need to be accomplished, and it is an enemy to perseverance when things are difficult. The longer hardships continue, the harder it is to be positive and devote the energy necessary to get through a crisis. War is no different. Soldiers, families, and the public all get weary of war. Sun Tzu recognized this about 2,500 years ago and left this keen insight.

> The main objective is a speedy resolution to the engagement. No matter how much planning you have done or how much money you have, a long drawn out conflict will exhaust your organization. Your troops will grow weary and lose their motivation and focus. They will lose their trust in you because it will be evident that you were unprepared.[90]

The only way to shorten a war is through the use of decisive action. That involves using maximum force to destroy resistance and reach objectives as quickly as possible. It's crucial to have public and political support for decisive action. When Clausewitz said, "The maximum use of force is in no way incompatible with the simultaneous use of the intellect," he was appealing to an understanding that maximum force shortens war and ultimately saves lives. And saving lives is the desire of moral nations.

Earlier, the United States's involvement in Somalia was discussed in relation to a lack of clearly defined objectives. The involvement in Somalia, from 1992 to 1994, also provides an illustration of how public opinion and political weakness curtail decisive action and cost lives. The defining moment of the US mission in Somalia happened on October 3–4, 1993. This was the date of the engagement portrayed in *Black Hawk Down*. US troops had been searching for

Mohamed Farrah Aidid since the end of August, led by Delta Force and Ranger units. The mission on October 3 was to capture Aidid's aides and officials at the Olympic Hotel in Mogadishu. The forces involved ran into trouble when they were ready to vacate the area. Somali militias blocked roads and attacked the convoy leaving the hotel. Two Black Hawk helicopters were shot down. By the end of a seventeen-hour battle, eighteen US servicemen were dead and over eighty were wounded. American commanders on the ground had assessed their situation and the assignment they had been given and had requested armor a month earlier. A *Frontline* chronology of the events that fall gave the following account of the handling of that request.

> In a decision that is later highly criticized, US Defense Secretary Les Aspin denies requests from General Montgomery for armored reinforcements, despite support for Montgomery's request from General Colin Powell. Aspin says that he did not want to create the appearance that the US was increasing forces in Somalia at a time when they were trying to reduce military presence. He later concedes, "Had I known at the time what I knew after the events of Sunday, [October 3]. I would have made a very different decision.[91]

Had he known. What a sad testimony for a defense secretary to give! He should have known what the consequences are for restricting force and failing to act decisively. Not only did the failure to give American troops the armor they needed cost American lives, but some estimates of Somali deaths that day run over one thousand. Tanks and armor are intimidating pieces of equipment. It's possible with armor assisting the operation that day there may have been no confrontation, and Somali lives could have been saved as well. *The whole point of a show of force is to avoid a confrontation.* The military is supposed to look intimidating. Personal defense classes teach individuals to walk with head up and confidence because it discourages criminal attack. The intent is not to look like a victim. The same principle is important in international relations. But in the exact opposite vein of thought, President Clinton, on October 7, 1993, ordered the search for Aidid stopped and the withdrawal of US forces from Somalia by March 31, 1994. That projected an image of weakness to the world that had deadly future consequences. And what was the main decision factor in denying armor? A concern of public and political opinion, resulting from creating the wrong appearance.

The fear over public and political response to the use of decisive force has reached a point that wars seldom actually end. They become ongoing engagements, without definitive decision, that result in continuing loss of life. In July of 2014, tensions flare into conflict again between Israel and Hamas in the Gaza Strip. From tunnels built with aid money donated by Israel, Hamas kidnapped and killed three Israeli teenagers. In the fifty-day conflict that followed, thousands of rockets were fired into Israel by Hamas as Israel carried out operations to destroy the tunnels within Gaza. Because of Israel's longtime efforts to minimize civilian casualties, Hamas uses schools, hospitals, and mosques to fire rockets from and hide weapons, knowing that Israel won't attack these areas. But is that the best way to save life and secure peace? Israel's recent history of indecisive action leaves the area in a constant state of conflict. Hamas only uses ceasefires to rearm and resupply for the next conflict, knowing they will be spared from a large-scale invasion that eliminates them as a military and political entity. Gaza has demonstrated its inability to be self-governing by supporting a terrorist organization as its ruling political party. Support for Hamas still seems to be high. A recent *Washington Post* article included this assessment: "According to the most recent polls, Hamas and its "military approach" are more popular than ever among Palestinians."[92] The question then becomes, at what point do the Palestinians become accountable for supporting and sustaining Hamas and its terror tactics?

Despite Israel's great care in avoiding civilian deaths, they do occur because of the dense population and the tactics of Hamas in hiding behind noncombatants. Israel even uses dud rockets to warn a building that it is targeted for attack. The dud will land on a roof long enough before the actual payload so that residents have enough time to escape. This practice is sometimes referred to as roof knocking. But these efforts have done little to change the view of Israel in the international eye, or solved the conflict with Hamas. Groups have condemned Israel for the destruction in Gaza during the summer of 2014 hostilities, including Amnesty International, United Nations Human Rights Council, and Physicians for Human Rights-Israel. To appease this criticism, Israel is conducting its own investigation into the prosecution of the summer war. Whatever they do, it won't be enough to satisfy those who don't understand what war is. This statement appeared in a *New York Times* article.

> Although Israel has expressed pride over its early-warning mechanisms, which include phone calls to residents of houses about to be bombed and fliers and nonexplosive missiles signaling an impending attack, the report concluded that they were inefficient. Only five of the 68 interviewees said they had received warnings. Those who did said no safe escape routes had been provided. Ten reported having been injured in a secondary strike.[93]

But there is very little international condemnation of Hamas for firing thousands of rockets into Israel. Israel faces a very difficult position in trying to prosecute a war against a terrorist enemy with indecisive action in an effort to appease international political correctness. They end up losing on both fronts. The cold truth is that as long as the citizens in Gaza are insulated from the consequences of supporting Hamas and its terrorism, public support for Hamas will remain high. As long as Hamas refuses to live peaceably with Israel the only solution for security in Gaza is a decisive campaign by Israel that eliminates resistance, occupies the area, and enforces security. The nation of Israel may not have the public or political will to do that, but until then, Gaza will remain a constant conflict with casualties on both sides.

Maximum force and decisive action are not pleasant to think about or witness. But the difficult path in this case is the path that reduces the loss of human life in the long term and creates a more peaceful world. It is paramount that the determination to act decisively is part of public understanding and political will.

Prosecute War Aggressively

Perhaps no other element has contributed to the death of more American soldiers in the last sixty-five years than the failure of America to prosecute wars aggressively. Closely tied to acting decisively, failing to prosecute war aggressively also lengthens the conflict and fails to bring about a conclusive victory. While acting decisively focuses on the maximum use of force, prosecuting aggressively directs attention to who the enemy is. Remember that victory is the submission of the defeated side to the *will* of the other. Within that statement, it is important to clarify whom it is that needs to submit. That may vary, depending on the circumstances of the conflict. At times, it may just be the opposing military or armed resistance that needs to submit as the general population may not be supportive of its current government.

That was the case in World War II in a somewhat strange twist of circumstances when the Nazis first invaded the Soviet Union. It is often overlooked or forgotten by those with just a casual interest in history that Soviet premier Joseph Stalin was as equally brutal a dictator as Hitler. In solidifying his power, he had put to death and starved millions. When the Germans entered Russia in the summer of 1941, the Wehrmacht was treated as a liberating army from Stalin's communist oppression. Ukrainians cheered the German soldiers and showered them with food. It was inevitable, however, that the Nazis would squander the good will given freely by the welcoming Russians. The fanatical, racist SS units and Reichskommissar that followed the German army quickly unleashed their brutality in the occupied territories and turned willing subjects into an army of partisans.

At other times, the population of a nation is either supportive of the actions of their government or willfully complacent. In those cases, it is the general population that must also submit to the will of the stronger side for victory to be achieved. Therein lies the sensitive question. Who is the enemy, and what force is needed to bring about submission? Chapter 3 of this book will examine how that question has been answered throughout past wars the United States has been involved in: where force was lacking, where force was used appropriately and inappropriately. In this section, a foundation will be laid for how to make that decision.

It's first necessary to understand who holds the ultimate power in a nation. It is the citizens of that nation. In America, that is recognized and stated within the preamble to the US Constitution with the introductory words: "We the People of the United States." But it is nevertheless true that ultimate power lies with the citizens in nations where repressive governments do not give any legal standing to the power or rights of the citizenry. It's true because every regime is susceptible to being overthrown by the mob. The ill-fated French Revolution (1787–1799) brought about the overthrow of Louis XVI and the French monarchy when the citizens of the nation rose up against that feudal system. The storming of the Bastille prison on July 14, 1789, is symbolic of the uprising. Dictators and tyrannical regimes fear the general population and often use brutal tactics to keep the masses divided against each other and controlled by fear. Governments are always dependent upon a population that is submissive to their rule. No government possesses enough security forces or can financially support enough security forces to control all the population at the same time by force.

Granted, it is not an easy thing for citizens to band together and overthrow a regime. For one reason, as Jefferson said in the Declaration of Independence "all experience hath shewn [sic], that mankind are more disposed to suffer, while evils are sufferable, than to right themselves by abolishing the forms to which they are accustomed." As long as enough citizens have their basic needs met and don't feel oppression too severely, they will more often submit to tyranny than rebel against it. Three factors are necessary for any uprising to succeed: unity, motivation, and organization. Those are difficult to bring together at the same time, but if present, they combine into an unstoppable force.

Machiavelli recognized the need for a government to have the will of the people to continue in power when he stated, "For however strong you may be in respect of your army, it is essential that in entering a new Province you should have the good will of its inhabitants."[94] Dabney is even more clear when he stated, "The truth is, that the physical power of even the most iron despotisms reposes on moral forces, and if these are withdrawn from beneath, the most rigid tyranny becomes but a *simulacrum*, which dissolves at the touch of resistance."[95] So the citizens of a nation, by support or complacency, cannot be held completely innocent of the actions of their government.

The term "total war" began to be popularized in the last half of the nineteenth century. Most sources today define total war as a war that is unrestricted in weapons used, who the combatants are, and objectives, and it disregards all rules of war. Some try and trace the origination of the concept back to Clausewitz, and although Clausewitz discussed the "pure concept" of war as an "absolute manifestation of violence," he spoke of it in theoretical terms and always stressed that war was a means to political objectives.[96] When Clausewitz spoke of war in limited and unlimited terms, he was referencing whether the objective was the total destruction of the enemies resistance so that any terms might be demanded or limited to something less. Clausewitz never advocated destruction for the sake of destruction. Genocides, such as that in Rwanda, are nothing more than organized murder but come closer to the definition most sources give of total war.

The Second World War typified total war in the respect that both sides viewed almost any property of the enemies as a legitimate target. At the other end of the spectrum is war as it was fought by some European armies in the eighteenth century. The conflict was decided by armies maneuvering on a field, engaging in battle, and ending when one general saw that he could not hold the field. The concept wasn't to destroy the opposing army as much as it was to win the battle and seek terms and settlements. That may have worked in times when nations were ruled by interrelated monarchies with subjects who accepted the will of the monarch. But as the political landscape shifted from monarchies to various forms of constitutional government, nationalism inspired more political will in the general population.

The Napoleonic wars began the shift to an objective of destroying the enemy's army. By the time of the American Civil War, old habits of being content to win the day were still engrained in some generals to the great frustration of Lincoln, who firmly believed the Southern armies must be destroyed to end the war. In a letter to President Lincoln dated July

7, 1862, General McClellan expressed his gentlemanly view of how the war should be conducted, even to the extent of maintaining the continued recognition of the property rights of slave owners. In summarizing his views, he said, "A system of policy thus constitutional, and pervaded by the influences of Christianity and freedom, would receive the support of almost all truly loyal men, would deeply impress the rebel masses and all foreign nations, and it might be humbly hoped that it would commend itself to the favor of the Almighty."[97] McClellan was gravely mistaken on the nature of the conflict he was engaged in. The "rebel masses" held deep convictions of fighting for the defense of their home and freedom of their state. It was going to take much more than McClellan's gentlemanly conflict to bring the South to a point of submitting to rejoining the Union. Clausewitz spoke with great foresight about the need to break the will of the enemy and the gruesome task it was. "Battle is the bloodiest solution….its effect…is rather a killing of the enemy's spirit than of his men."[98]

By the end of 1864, as the Confederate armies courageously and stubbornly continued to fight on in the midst of overwhelming odds and severe shortages of supplies, William Tecumseh Sherman set out across Georgia on a campaign to make all the South sick of war. Sherman wired to the war department: "If the people raise a howl against barbarity and cruelty, I will answer that war is war, and not popularity seeking. We are not only fighting hostile armies, but a hostile people, and must make old and young, rich and poor, feel the hard hand of war."[99] A month earlier in October, Sheridan's army had set about destroying crops and livestock in the Shenandoah Valley of Virginia to rob the South of resources to continue the fight. The harsh tactics of Sherman and Sheridan contributed to ending the war and bringing the southern states back into the Union without a long period of continued guerrilla warfare that plagues so many other nations torn by Civil War. It was the weakness and starvation of Lee's men at Appomattox that prompted the surrender. If the Army of Northern Virginia had been strong and well fed, many more lives would have been lost that April before the war came to an end. In Robert Dabney's preface to Stonewall Jackson's biography, he expresses his own resignation and submission to the will of the Northern victors.

> But I am ready to add, with equal candor, that when I thus declare boldly the principles upon which the Virginians of 1861 acted, I do not intend to be understood as retracting that acquiescence in the result of the arbitrament of the sword, and that submission promised by me in common with almost the whole South. I have voluntarily sworn to obey the government of the United States, as at present established and expounded to us by force of arms. That oath it is my purpose to keep.[100]

Total war, as it is defined today, is wrong. No purpose is served by indiscriminate killing of civilians or destruction of property not related to contributing to an enemy's war effort. But neither is it feasible in war to only target combatants and believe that alone will bring about the submission of the enemy. A plan to prosecute war aggressively requires a careful analysis of who the enemy is. As Sherman said, all the enemy must be made to feel "the hard hand of war" in some way. The goal is to save lives by bringing a quick end to the war, and war only ends when those who support it see that the consequences are too great to continue. Those who harbor and give aid to combatants need to know they put their own lives at risk by being in proximity to them. Accomplices to combatants are combatants. Infrastructure that contributes to war production or continuance is also a legitimate target. Actions that disrupt or eliminate the financial ability of an enemy to conduct war are important steps to take. Even food and water supplies are legitimate targets. Every human being is subject to the needs of food, water, and sleep. Take these away, and the strongest enemy becomes weak. These actions will be hard on the population of the enemy nation. But citizens cannot be immune from the consequences of the actions of their government. The military value of a target cannot always be set aside upon consideration of civilian casualties. The question to ask is, how many lives will be lost if this target *isn't* destroyed?

When wars aren't prosecuted aggressively, they continue on and lives are lost. Enemies are encouraged and reinforced by timidity in their opponent. War isn't a refereed sporting event. It is a life-and-death struggle, and it needs to be ended as quickly as possible. All the enemy, citizens, and combatants need to feel that the fight is hopeless. The fastest way to accomplish that is to aggressively attack and destroy anything that contributes to a sense of optimism in the war effort. That is difficult to do, and it takes foresight to see that it is the most humane thing to do. Clausewitz recognized that it is a difficult truth for military commanders to accept. He said, "It is always true that the character of battle, like its name, is slaughter [Schlacht], and its price is blood. As a human being the commander will recoil from it."[101]

Clausewitz was a veteran of many campaigns, but the brutality of war wasn't lost to him. He was with the Russians pursuing the French on their desperate retreat from Moscow in 1812. Napoleon had entered Russia at the end of June 1812 with an army of around five hundred thousand men, expecting to make quick work of the much smaller Russian army. But the Russians, in a brilliant defensive strategy, refused to commit to a decisive battle. Instead, they slowly withdrew before the French, burning everything as they retreated to deprive the French of any Russian provisions. Famine, disease, summer heat, desertions, and the wounded from the small battles fought along the way—these took their toll on Napoleon's army. Fighting in early September near Moscow cost tens of thousands of casualties. Again, the Russians retreated and abandoned Moscow, but with the Russian army and government intact, it was a hollow victory for Napoleon.

By October 19, 1812, with winter approaching and no supplies, the approximately one hundred thousand French left began a retreat for Europe. Now the Russian army went on the offensive, forcing the French to fight as they went. At the Berezina River, the Russians were in position to deal the French a final blow. Admiral Chichagov was on the west side of the river. To the north was General Wittgenstein, with Field Marshal Kutuzov and the main Russian force a few days behind to the east. By this time, the French army was reduced to sixty to seventy thousand men. A valiant effort by French engineers created two hasty bridges to attempt a crossing in late November. The chaos and panic that ensued left thousands more dead. Wittgenstein held the key to delaying the French at the river, but for some reason, he didn't aggressively attack. In a letter to his wife, Clausewitz described with great sorrow the carnage at the Berezina River. Yet he also understood the opportunity lost there by the Russians. In speaking of General Wittgenstein, he said, "He might have made the French loss much greater."[102]

Was it compassion that prevented Wittgenstein from throwing everything at the French? The French were in a desperate position: poor defensive ground, a difficult crossing, and fighting on both sides of the river. The effort that Wittgenstein did throw at Napoleon forced him at one point to send troops back to the east side to reinforce his rearguard. An all-out effort by Wittgenstein may have allowed Chichagov to completely stop the crossing on the west side and allowed Kutuzov time to bring up the rest of the army and annihilate the French. Would that bloodshed have been worth it? What was lost in the French escaping?

The Napoleonic wars didn't hinge on occupying territory or taking an enemy capital. They hinged on a man, Napoleon. Capturing or killing Napoleon would end the wars. At Berezina, the Russians had an opportunity to do just that. At the moment, it may have seemed cruel and senseless to slaughter the remaining weakened French, but they were far fewer than those that were yet to die when Napoleon rebuilt an army and continued the war. One writer expressed it this way: "Nonetheless, the extraordinary performance and sacrifice of so many in the French army enabled it to continue to exist and have a framework from which to *build a new army* [italics mine] in the coming months."[103]

It may be recalled that a somewhat similar circumstance occurred after the Battle of Fredericksburg in the American Civil War. General Burnside's troops were trapped in a stalemate on the south side of the Rappahannock River after the battle on December 13, 1862. At sunset of that day, Confederate General Jackson drew up orders for a night assault to throw the federals back into the river and create a great slaughter. The order was withdrawn, but the Confederates were anxious for an opportunity to destroy the Union army. What is illustrative in comparing this event to the Russians at the Berezina is looking at the reasons why destroying the enemy army was so important. *The key to knowing when to act aggressively is understanding the enemy and what will bring about submission and victory.* In the Napoleonic wars, it was eliminating Napoleon. For Lincoln and the Union, it was bringing all the population of the south into submission. But for the Confederacy, it was simply causing the Union to get tired of fighting. Destroying the federal army at Fredericksburg would have given a greater voice to those in the North who already viewed the war as to costly. By contrast, if the South would have been able to invade the North and destroy crops and industry, it may have been counterproductive by solidifying Union support and resolve for the war. So aggressive prosecution of a war is not an indiscriminate act of total war that targets everything but a carefully laid-out strategy based on clearly defined objectives and an understanding of the enemy.

Kindness at the wrong moment can kill. A determination to prosecute wars aggressively is an essential element of public opinion and political will so that future lives can be saved. At times, it is necessary to accept responsibility for the brutality of the moment and see the peace that it can bring about. Clearly defined, realistic objectives, an astute understanding of who the enemy is, and the public and political support of a nation give commanders the tools to know when those moments present themselves. Wars can end. And lives will be saved on both sides.

Persevere

America has the best trained, most technologically advanced, military in the world. There is no nation that can compete with United States productivity. America is one of the wealthiest nations in natural resources, and America led the world in founding a nation on morally superior ideals. Geographically, the United States is naturally defended on two sides by oceans, a friendly ally to the north and, excepting the security issues on its southern border, a cooperative ally to the south. Where does the weakness in America's security lie? It lies in maintaining the resolve necessary to see conflicts through to victory. Even if public opinion and political will possess the determination to be prepared, act before a crisis, clearly define realistic objectives, act decisively, and prosecute war aggressively, without perseverance, wars will end with questions over what was accomplished, the purpose of the soldiers' sacrifice, and a shaken confidence in the leadership of the nation or America itself. America doesn't lose wars; the history of the last decades reveal America usually just quits and goes home. It is easy to grow weary of war when political leadership fails to clearly define realistic objectives or act decisively and prosecute aggressively. The American people instinctively know soldiers die needlessly because of foolish political correctness. But there is a definite need for perseverance to see conflicts through to victory. Out of the vast experience of Clausewitz, came this observation.

> In war more than anywhere else things do not turn out as we expect.... *Perseverance* in the chosen course is the essential counterweight, provided that no compelling reasons intervene to the contrary. Moreover, there is hardly a worthwhile enterprise in war whose execution does not call for infinite effort, trouble, and privation; and as man under pressure tends to give in to physical and intellectual weakness, only great strength of will can lead to the objective. It is steadfastness that will earn the admiration of the world and of posterity.[104]

That same steadfastness needed by the soldier on the line is required of the nation at home. But it is difficult. Everyone wants war to end. As casualties mount and setbacks occur, questions arise if the nation is on the right course. The clearly defined, realistic objective is crucial at this point. Understanding strengthens resolve. The temptation to quit is always present and is the hope of the enemy. The strongest leaders are not immune to its pressure.

President Lincoln had his finger on the pulse of the nation when he prepared his Gettysburg address. The horrifying casualty numbers from the fighting in July continued to embolden the Northern antiwar faction. Should the Union quit fighting and seek a peaceful recognition of the independence of the Confederate states? Two things helped Lincoln to stay the course, which he emphasized in his speech. They were the objective of "a new birth of freedom," to make the principles of equality expressed in the Declaration of Independence a reality in law and a consideration of those who had sacrificed all for the cause thus far. How does it honor the sacrifice of those already dead to quit before victory? Those who lay down their life in war deserve that their sacrifice is a step forward to the goal. Hence, Lincoln made his stirring appeal "that these dead shall not have died in vain."

Throughout the next summer of 1864, General Grant attacked without letup the Confederacy. Grant was finally a general who was willing to use the enormous material advantage of the Union to attempt to destroy Lee's army. However, the casualties were horrific. The year 1864 was an election year as well. The Democratic party platform called for peace with the Confederacy, which meant a continuation of slavery. They had selected as their candidate Lincoln's former commander of the Army of the Potomac, George McClellan. Although McClellan publicly stated he would continue the war, his vice presidential candidate was an opponent to the war, and it is difficult to see how he could have continued the war without the support of his party. Lincoln's prospects for reelection did not look good that summer. The nation was weary of war. By August, with the news from the front all discouraging, even Lincoln's resolve was shaken. On August 24, 1864, he drafted a letter instructing Henry Raymond to go and offer terms of peace to Jefferson Davis. The terms were simply that the southern states return to the Union with slavery and other issues to be resolved by peaceful means.[105] Those peaceful means obviously would have involved legislation in Congress, which, with the return of the southern states, meant that slavery would have continued. The Emancipation Proclamation was a wartime document that would need to be codified by law in some way to truly abolish slavery. That wasn't accomplished until the adoption of the thirteenth amendment in 1865. Fortunately, the president never sent the letter, and the next day, his courage and resolve to continue the war had returned.

The illustration of such a man as President Lincoln being tempted to quit shows how difficult it can be to persevere in times of great trial. In September of 1864, news of Atlanta falling into Union hands began to turn the tide of the election. And with Lincoln's reelection, the hopes of the South dimmed. But they had come very close to bringing the Union to the point of quitting the conflict. The United States quitting a conflict is still the greatest ally and hope its enemies have. Very few nations can match the material advantages of the United States. If there is a determination to use the resources and military advantage the United States possesses, there is little hope of victory for any opponent. Unfortunately, over the decades, most enemies of America have learned that all they have to do is wait for the Americans to leave.

Walking away from a conflict in which soldiers have lost their lives is discouraging to the families of the fallen, the morale of the military, and the confidence of the nation. But another casualty of quitting a conflict is America's standing in the world and ability to form alliances in future conflicts. America needs to be known as a nation that keeps its promises. In the years that America has been in Afghanistan, efforts were made to gain the cooperation of the various tribes and groups against the Taliban. Those who aided America put their lives and families at great risk. Now with America ending its combat role there, who is going to protect those who sacrificed to help the US effort? Is the Afghan army able to provide that security? How does the United States gain cooperation in the future from nationals if they are left on their own when the United States decides to leave? These are difficult questions. All Americans are tired of the long war in Afghanistan. But the reality is that a US presence there is going to be necessary to support the current Afghan government. That role can and should shift to continued training and support. Like Iraq, it will take at least a generation seeing a strong central government and a peaceful, secure nation before true stability can be expected. Part of the blame for the difficult situation is the lack of a realistic objective at the start of the war. Long wars are never easy, and it is imperative to have realistic goals at the start and prosecute them aggressively to minimize time involved in a conflict. Perseverance is always easier when everyone knows what the end looks like and can see it getting closer.

A policy is a principle of action. Six foundational elements are necessary for a successful war policy, one that saves American lives, minimizes enemy casualties, and results in victory. These elements are foundational because the heart and soul of the nation need to grab hold of them before one boot steps on enemy ground. These elements transcend time and constitute an understanding of the reality of war and human nature. No life should be lost in vain. To prevent that, America must have the determination to

- Be prepared
- Act before a crisis
- Clearly define realistic objectives
- Act decisively
- Prosecute war aggressively
- Persevere

Is any life truly lost in vain when it's lost in service to country? From the perspective of what was accomplished by the mission, or war, it is right to think of it in those terms to learn and be more cautious and prudent in future engagements. But from the aspect of the human tragedy involved, the answer is no. No life is lost in vain in service to country. Every American citizen owes their deepest respect and gratitude to every person who has served in uniform and their deepest heartfelt sympathy, compassion, and honor to those who have fallen and their families. The political failures of national leadership that gives up what soldiers have gained doesn't take away from the honor America has for its service members.

Among the papers found in General Lee's army satchel after his death was this handwritten note. Although nothing can take away the grief or loss felt by the families of the fallen, it is a fitting tribute of honor from a grateful nation to its heroes.

> The warmest instincts of every man's soul declare the glory of the soldier's death. It is more appropriate to the Christian than to the Greek to sing: 'Glorious his fate, and envied is his lot, Who for his country fights and for it dies.' There is a true glory and a true honor; the glory of duty done—the honor of the integrity of principle.[106]

3

Learning from History

History isn't a mystical crystal ball that unlocks the secrets of the future. It is simply a story, a story of humanity. What makes history relevant is that human beings do not change, unfortunately. Human nature is the same now as it has always been, and mankind responds to similar circumstances and events in the same manner. Machiavelli's *The Prince* is intriguing because of its remarkable insight into human nature; it is just as germane today as it was five hundred years ago. To learn from history is to learn about people. That information can be used for good or evil. It can be used to recognize egotistic, charismatic leaders and take warning about what similar individuals have done in the past. It can be used by such leaders to manipulate a nation, or it can be used to save lives. Learning from history as it pertains to a successful war policy is to learn how one side in a conflict can quickly be brought to submitting to the will of the other side, and the war can end.

Winston Churchill is a very interesting and captivating individual in history. His keen insight into the nature of the enemy Britain faced in the Second World War was instrumental in the preservation of the nation, and his insight into human nature was also a powerful asset in motivating the nation on to victory in the war. The following quote, taken from an address to the House of Commons on May 2, 1935, demonstrates his understanding of human nature and recognizes the consequence that comes from failing to learn from its display in history. His remarks are also quite prescient about Britain's future.

> When the situation was manageable it was neglected, and now that it is thoroughly out of hand we apply too late the remedies which then might have effected a cure. There is nothing new in the story. It is as old as the sibylline books. It falls into that long, dismal catalogue of the fruitlessness of experience and the confirmed unteachability of mankind. Want of foresight, unwillingness to act when action would be simple and effective, lack of clear thinking, confusion of counsel until the emergency comes, until self-preservation strikes its jarring gong–these are the features which constitute the endless repetition of history.[107]

- That These Dead -

The Second World War was the largest war in human history in terms of nations involved, the size of the armies, length of battle lines, geographic scope, and the number of dead. Casualty figures for any war or battle are always subject to the source. Numbers for the dead from World War II range from thirty-five million in combat to seventy-five million with civilians included. Those are staggering numbers. It's difficult to process that amount of death. It was a relatively short war, six years. Yet to reach seventy-five million dead in six years, over thirty-four thousand people would have to be slaughtered per day. Entire cities were obliterated. But it was a war that had to be fought. The unchecked aggression of Germany and Japan would have left a world in the grip of evil and an unimaginable horror for its inhabitants. On the part of the Axis powers, it was total war in its ugliest form; and at times, that line was crossed in the targets the Allies chose. But it was a war that was prosecuted to win, part of the reason it only lasted six years. It was fought with the attitude that wars should be fought with an all-out determination to throw everything at the enemies and bring them to defeat.

In the first years of the war, because of the unpreparedness of the Allies, it was a struggle for survival. But as the tide began to turn and the American war industry turned out massive amounts of military hardware, the focus shifted to the offensive. In mid-January 1943, President Roosevelt and

Prime Minister Churchill met in Casablanca, Morocco. Their topic of discussion was the consolidation of war plans for after the North Africa campaign was finished. Stalin, who didn't attend the meetings, was still insistent that the British and Americans open a second front against Germany in France. To have a chance for success, the invasion of France would have to wait for a larger buildup of forces in England and air superiority over the *Luftwaffe*. That wasn't realistic until 1944, but Roosevelt and Churchill did agree to open a front against Italy by the summer of 1943, with a landing at Sicily.

Perhaps the greatest outcome of the conference came in an unplanned remark by Roosevelt. At a press conference on January 24, Roosevelt said, "Peace can come to the world only by the total elimination of German and Japanese war power.…The elimination of German, Japanese, and Italian war power means the unconditional surrender of Germany, Italy and Japan."[108] If Roosevelt did plan to make the demand of an unconditional surrender, it wasn't discussed with the British beforehand. It created a stir at the time and continues to be a source of debate with historians whether the remark increased the resolve of the Axis powers. It did solidify the thought that the evil the Allies were fighting against could not be dealt with and left to survive; it must be destroyed. The war was fought with just such determination. For America, at least, the phrase "unconditional surrender" was a clear objective of what was being fought for.

On May 10, 1940, the hope of the French and British that the Germans were content with the conquest of Poland came to an abrupt end when the German blitzkrieg moved west. The Germans sent their swift-moving panzer divisions, which were supported by the superior *Luftwaffe*, crashing through the Ardennes of southern Belgium. Other divisions launched attacks along the German border through the Netherlands. The plan was to drive through Belgium and the Netherlands to the sea, avoid the heavier defenses of the French along the Maginot Line, and attack France from the north. Despite the German army actually being smaller than the combined forces of the Allies in Western Europe, the German plan worked brilliantly. The superior tactics and leadership of the Germans led to a swift victory. At the end of May and first few days of June, a miraculous evacuation off the beaches at Dunkirk rescued over three hundred thousand surviving British and French troops. Fortunately, Hitler restrained his panzers from closing on Dunkirk and believed he could halt the evacuation from the air. He was wrong, and the courage of British civilians who used almost any private boat they could find saved the British Army from annihilation. By June 5, the German army turned its attention south to finish the conquest of France, and on June 14, Paris was occupied. Three days later, France asked for armistice terms.

These shocking turn of events left England alone. At the time, Britain was still a colonial power. British troops were stationed from northern Africa, through the Middle East to

India, and reaching as far as Hong Kong. Britain would soon be fighting all three Axis powers: Germany, Italy, and Japan. That is if it survived 1940. After the fall of France, there was an immediate fear that the Nazis would quickly set about invading England. Hitler's war machine, while to this point unstoppable on land, was not prepared for an amphibious assault on England. The German navy was still weaker than the British fleet, and though outnumbered, the Royal Air Force would be an obstacle to any attempted invasion. Hitler hoped the British would sue for peace, but he underestimated the free spirit of the British inspired by Winston Churchill. The first step to any such invasion by Germany would be to gain air superiority by destroying the RAF, and so an air war began over England that is known as the Battle of Britain.

An air raid on some docks on July 10, 1940, is given as the starting date for the Battle of Britain in history books. For eleven months, until June of 1941, German planes pound first military targets and then London and civilian targets. The Battle of Britain provides a view into a population's response to the needless attack of civilians and the choice of targets in a war. Victory in any war is the submission of one side to the will of the other. It is crucial to know what events will bring about that submission. The key to bringing about submission in the enemy is to create a feeling of hopelessness about the war. That is much different than creating a feeling of hopelessness of life or creating feelings of hostility and hatred. That distinction was thankfully lost on the Germans as they attempted to cause the British to resign themselves to defeat and ask for peace.

In the German's first attacks against Britain, they concentrated on military targets and specifically the RAF. August was a frightful month as the Germans hit radar stations, airfields, and ground communication systems for the RAF. The RAF fighter pilots were the primary defense against the German attacks and suffered heavy losses. By the end of August, it was beginning to look like Goring's *Luftwaffe* might succeed in destroying Britain's fighter defenses. Had that happened, it would have been a twofold blow—one to the actual ability of Britain to defend herself and another to the morale of the people, having the effect of creating a hopelessness over the war. But again, Hitler changed tactics. On August 24, some German planes on a night mission against an airfield mistakenly dropped some of their bombs on part of London. This prompted a small effort by the British to bomb Berlin. Hitler was infuriated and shifted the air war over Britain from the objective of destroying the RAF to bombing London. On September 7, 1940, the bombing of London began. It didn't have the effect Hitler wanted.

Hitler's efforts to destroy London and the morale of the British people had the effect of strengthening the resolve of the British to completely defeat their Nazi foe. As has been discussed, no nation can continue without at least the complacency of its citizens, and it is equally difficult to be successful in war without public support. In the last days of the Confederacy, General Lee was made commander in chief of all the Confederate forces. Previously, he was the commander of the Army of Northern Virginia. In a general order dated February 9, 1865, he made this statement that addressed the need for the continued support of the South. "Deeply impressed with the difficulties and responsibilities of the position, and humbly invoking the guidance of Almighty God, I rely for success upon the courage and fortitude of the Army, *sustained by the patriotism and firmness of the people*, confident that their *united efforts*, under the blessing of Heaven, will secure peace and independence"[109] (italics mine). Lee recognized the need for the continued support of the southern population to have any hope of success in the war. A goal of war should always be to undermine and eliminate any public support the enemy enjoys from its citizens. That can be difficult to do, and every situation is unique in the best way to accomplish that. The object is to create hopelessness in the right place. The enemy must be made to believe that things would be better if the war ended. Hitler's attacks on London and the British citizens only had the effect of solidifying his evil in the minds of the British. It was a foretaste of what would come with a Nazi victory, and it only strengthened British resolve. However, a continued effort by Germany to destroy the RAF may have kept the British focused and worried about losing the war and taken away a belief that victory was possible. People should always be left with the hope that things can be better, and that hope should believe the better comes with the war's end. Machiavelli said it this way:

> Those cruelties we may say are well employed, if it be permitted to speak well of things evil, which are done once for all under the necessity of self-preservation, and are not afterwards persisted in, but so far as possible modified to the advantage of the governed.... but be enabled by their discontinuance [cruelties] to reassure men's minds, and afterwards win them over by benefits.[110]

The United States has rightfully done a good job in always extending kindness to the population of enemy nations. The recent wars in Iraq and Afghanistan are a testament to the commitment of the United States to help these nations by building infrastructure, utilities, schools, and the foundations for an improved standard of living. But often the United States has failed to create consequences for support of the enemy. To be effective in winning over support of the population of enemy nations, a choice must be presented: hopelessness for aiding the enemy or opportunity for supporting peace.

The Battle of Britain also illustrates the need to stay focused on military targets. Later in the war, the Allies forgot how quickly they were able to recover from the damage inflicted by an attack and overestimated the damage inflicted by Allied raids on Germany. The *Luftwaffe* was constantly surprised, despite attacks on aircraft factories and the number of British planes destroyed, at the number of planes Britain was able to put in the air. The resiliency of the RAF, coupled with the strategic blunder of Hitler in shifting strikes away from the RAF to civilian targets, cost Germany a chance to dramatically change the outcome of the war. But Germany wasn't the only side to make that mistake in the war.

Albert Speer began his association with the Third Reich as an architect. Hitler was an amateur artist and wishful architect. In fact, as Speer later said, "Amateurishness was one of Hitler's dominant traits."[111] Speer joined the Nazi party in 1931 after hearing Hitler speak at Berlin University. In 1932, he did some work for Joseph Goebbels constructing the district headquarters for the party in Berlin. In July of 1933, Speer presented designs for background architecture to Hitler for the upcoming party rally to be held at Nuremberg. That was his first personal meeting with Hitler, but it began an extremely close working relationship that lasted to the end of the war in 1945. Hitler had grand plans for the design of a future Berlin that would portray the magnificence of his Reich. In Speer, he found an architect and person with whom he could share his passion for building his grand designs.

While Speer was working on the chancellor's residence, Hitler invited Speer to dinner one evening and later expressed this sentiment about the invitation.

> You attracted my notice during our rounds. I was looking for an architect to whom I could entrust my building plans. I wanted someone young; for as you know these plans extend far into the future. I need someone who will be able to continue after my death with the authority I have conferred on him. I saw you as that man.[112]

In February of 1942, Albert Speer's duties to Hitler took on a different nature with the death of Dr. Todt, the armaments minister, in a plane crash. Speer was appointed minister of armaments and war production among other duties that Todt had. Although he didn't have any experience with weapons or the military, his brilliant analytical, organizational, logistical, and managerial skills allowed him to accomplish amazing feats with armament production. Despite the tremendous air assault on Germany, production numbers of small arms continued to increase from 1943 to 1944. Average rifles produced per month in 1943 were 209,000. Production for November 1944 was 307,000. Ammunition for the rifles rose from 203,000,000 rounds per month in 1943 to 486,000,000 rounds produced in November 1944. Other astonishing numbers were displayed in production of planes and tanks up to the last few months of the war. This wasn't lost on the Allies as in Britain, *The Observer* gave this assessment of Speer in an article April 9, 1944.

> Speer is, in a sense, more important for Germany today than Hitler, Himmler, Goering, Goebbels, or the generals. They all have, in a way, become the mere auxiliaries of the man who actually directs the giant power machine—charged with drawing from it the maximum effort under maximum strain....In him is the very epitome of the "managerial revolution."[113]

This new position gave Speer an inside knowledge of the effects of Allied bombings of Germany. Often, the Allies were sporadic in their focus on military targets just as the Germans had been in the Battle of Britain. With the advantage of working within the armament industry, Speer knew just how devastating to the war effort a concentrated attack on a single aspect of the war could be. After urging Hitler to instruct the *Luftwaffe* to use pinpoint attacks against vital enemy military targets as late as 1943 to no avail, Speer made this comment in reference to the failure of Germany against England earlier. "There is no question that once before he had thrown away his chance—between 1939 and 1941 when he directed our air raids against England's cities instead of coordinating them with the U-boat campaigns and, for example, attacking the English ports which were in any case sometimes strained beyond their capacity by the convoy system."[114]

In his memoirs, Speer references three separate incidences in which the Allies could have significantly shortened the war if they had but continued a concentrated effort against a vital military target. The first was a May 1943 attack by the

RAF on the hydroelectric plants in the Ruhr. One out of four dams was destroyed in a single effort, but the British failed to follow up on knocking out vital electric power and water supplies for German industry. A second incident he mentions is the bombing of the ball bearing factory at Schweinfurt. The first raid at Schweinfurt was August 17, 1943, followed by another raid on October 14. Losses for the American air force were heavy since they had to make a portion of the trip without fighter escort. Attacks in December and more in February 1944 on the ball bearing industry reduced output by over 70 percent. But Speer comments, "At the beginning of April 1944, however, the attacks on the ball-bearing industry ceased abruptly. Thus, the Allies threw away success when it was already in their hands. Had they continued the attacks of March and April with the same energy, we would quickly have been at our last gasp."[115] The third incident he mentions is the attacks on fuel production that began on May 12, 1944. These attacks were sustained better and forced the Germans to divert hundreds of thousands of workers to rebuilding and maintaining the fuel industry.

In a paper published by the American Economic Warfare Division on December 9, 1942, the following statement was made: "Better to cause a high degree of destruction in a few really essential industries or services than to cause a small degree of destruction in many industries."[116] That is still important advice to follow in prosecuting a war. It isn't always as easy to put into practice. As in the case of the attacks on

Germany's ball bearing industry, the losses in American aircraft and crew were so severe at first that it wasn't possible to sustain that level of effort against them. Often, damage estimates were exaggerated, and a plant thought to be destroyed was quickly put back into operation. Sustained, consistent attacks were required to keep industry from coming back. People were amazingly resilient. Destruction was rebuilt, and economies naturally started back up. Just twelve days after the first atomic bomb was dropped on Hiroshima, the Yokohama Specie Bank was open for business in the center of the ruined city, operating out of a wood stall on the first floor of what was left of the building.[117]

The air war against Germany consisted of many direct raids against civilian centers with no military value. According to Speer, it had about the same effect as the bombing of London had on the British. Speer commented that the civilian raids seemed to increase determination and productivity, which emphasizes the point that the goal is to create hopelessness in continuing the war, not a despair of life. Utilities, communications, transportation, and economic industry that can be used in the war effort (which does include a wide scope) are legitimate targets if they contribute to creating that hopelessness. But random destruction and killing of civilians rarely produces the desired effect. Perhaps the greatest tragedy in the air war over Europe happened on February 13–15, 1945. Starting the night of the thirteenth, the city of Dresden was bombed. Horrific fires raged in a city that was crowded with refugees from the eastern front. The city was virtually leveled, and the death toll was staggering. Estimates run from thirty-five thousand up to over one hundred thousand. Sadly, there wasn't any military value to Dresden. One writer said, "Dresden, a beautiful and ancient city, was known for its production of porcelain dolls, not military weapons."[118]

Was it right then to drop the atomic bombs on Hiroshima and Nagasaki? The answer to that question provides an example of how important it is to know the nature of the enemy so that aggressive force can be used at the right place and time to bring about submission. As the US forces moved closer to Japan, fighting on Iwo Jima and Okinawa revealed what fighting would be like on mainland Japan. Japanese soldiers were dug into tunnels and hidden positions and rarely surrendered, choosing rather to fight to the death. At Okinawa, kamikaze attacks (Japanese pilots flying planes loaded with explosives into American ships and targets) number in the hundreds and sink over thirty ships. Taking the island claimed the lives of 12,500 Americans, 120,000 Japanese soldiers, and 42,000 civilians.[119] The civilian losses were almost 10 percent of the population. A veteran of the First Marine Division who fought on Peleliu and Okinawa made this statement about what it was like fighting the Japanese.

> The war I knew was totally savage… Our attitude towards the Japanese was different than the one we had toward the Germans. My brother who was with

the Second Infantry Division in the Battle of the Bulge, wounded three times, said when things were hopeless for the Germans, they surrendered... When they surrendered, they were guys just like us. With the Japanese, it was not that way.[120]

At the end of June 1945, when the fighting on Okinawa was over, the closest main Japanese island was still 350 miles away. The Japanese had large numbers of troops still in China and Southeast Asia that could be recalled to defend the homeland. The prospect of fighting over every inch of Japan as was required at Okinawa would have cost a catastrophic number of lives. Projections of American casualties for an invasion of just the southernmost island were 268,000 in dead and wounded.[121] The war could have continued for several years with millions of military and civilian deaths. The question to answer in deciding to use the new atomic bomb was, how many will die if it *isn't* used?

As horrible as the destruction and loss of life was at Hiroshima and Nagasaki, it was the right decision and it saved American and Japanese lives. That doesn't change the horror and pain brought by the atomic bomb. In John Hersey's book *Hiroshima*, he gives the detailed account of the experiences of six survivors of the first atomic bomb. It's a story of great courage and compassion; it accurately details the great suffering as well. As one survivor was trying to move an injured woman, "[h]e reached down and took a woman by the hands, but her skin slipped off in huge, glovelike pieces."[122] Another survivor described the scene of about twenty soldiers who may have been manning an antiaircraft battery looking up in the sky when the bomb went off: "They were all in exactly the same nightmarish state: their faces were wholly burned, their eye sockets were hollow, the fluid from their melted eyes had run down their cheeks."[123] The incendiary bombs dropped earlier on Tokyo were just as bad, creating fires that snuffed out almost one hundred thousand lives.

If only everyone was touched by such suffering, there might not be war again; but evil exists, and it must be stopped. War is horrible. The only way it becomes less so is when it ends, and the atomic bombs ended the war with Japan.

One other observation that will be made here concerning the Second World War concerns nation-building. Perhaps because World War II was so successful in terms of defeating the enemy, and Germany and Japan becoming strong allies over the years, it may be taken for granted that it always works that way. A contributing factor to the defeat of the Axis was adherence to the elements for a successful war policy that have just been highlighted. There was a clear objective, decisive action was taken, the war was prosecuted aggressively, and the Allies were committed to persevering until the objective of unconditional surrender was reached. Nation-building, with Germany and Japan becoming democratic peaceful allies, was possible because of unique circumstances. It is never easy or even possible to be successful in nation-building. Machiavelli observed this about human nature in regard to establishing a new government. "This lukewarm temper arises...partly from the incredulity of mankind, who will never admit the merit of anything new, until they have seen it proved by the event."[124] So in postwar Germany (west), even though a new democratic government was established, there was a shared historical and cultural background with other western democracies that went back centuries. This contributed to the integration of Germany into the western alliances. Japan presented a different unique circumstance that made a new nation possible. That was the devotion and submission to the wishes of the emperor.

It was that same devotion that made the bombings of Hiroshima and Nagasaki effective in ending the war. Normally, civilian bombings only strengthen the resolve of the enemy. But in this case, the destruction was so complete with the effort of only one plane and bomb that it created the realization to the emperor that to continue the war would mean the end of Japan. Throughout the 1930s, the military in Japan had seized control of more and more of the government culminating in 1940 when General Hideki Tojo became prime minister. The emperor had little to do with the day-to-day operation of the government but was still looked to as the final authority over Japan. After the atomic bombings, the Supreme War Council of Japan met to discuss surrender. There was much deliberation but no agreement. Finally, it was decided to leave the decision to the emperor. It was he who said, "I cannot bear to see my innocent people suffer any longer," and wished to accept the terms of surrender.[125] At the emperor's word, the people surrendered and submitted to the efforts of the United States to build a new nation. A survivor of Hiroshima gave this touching and revealing statement that explains the overnight transformation of Japan from hostile to peaceful and cooperative.

> At the time of the Post-War, the marvelous thing in our history happened. Our Emperor broadcasted his own voice through radio directly to us, common people of Japan. Aug. 15th we were told that some news of great importance could be heard & all of us should hear it. So I went to Hiroshima railway station. There set a loudspeaker in the ruins of the station. Many civilians, all of them were in boundage, some being helped by shoulder of their daughters, some sustaining their injured feet by sticks, they listened to the broadcast and when they came to realize the fact that it was the Emperor, they cried with full tears in their eyes, 'What a wonderful blessing it is that Tenno himself call on us and we can hear his own voice in person. We are thoroughly satisfied in such a great sacrifice.' When they came to know the war was ended—that is, Japan was defeated, they, of course, were deeply disappointed, but followed after their Emperor's commandment in calm spirit, making whole-hearted sacrifice for the everlasting peace of the world—and Japan started her new way."[126]

A few select events from the Second World War have been looked at that give insight to some of the elements of war that brought such a successful conclusion to that conflict and also some mistakes that were made. There is perhaps no other foreign war in American history that had such a clear objective and reasons why America was fighting. That created a tremendous spirit of unity and effort on the home front that was indispensable to the soldiers overseas and to producing the quantities of material necessary to win. It truly was an amazing effort, and the world still owes a debt of gratitude to that generation. Sterling Mace, who was also with the First Marine Division on Peleliu and Okinawa lost a dear friend on Peleliu. Before he left the island, while visiting his friend's grave and looking over the First Division cemetery, he made this comment, "At least they didn't die for nothing. People do that—'die for nothing'—back in the States all the time, but they'll care about these boys of Peleliu forever."[127] Yes, America has not forgotten. She still cares and thanks them.

In August of 1941, President Roosevelt and Prime Minister Churchill met off the coast of Newfoundland aboard two of their respective navy's war ships: the HMS *Prince of Wales* and USS *Augusta*. Even though the United States was not officially at war yet, the two leaders met to discuss the aims of the war and what they would like the world to look like after it was over. An eight-point document known as the Atlantic

Charter was drafted that has had far-reaching consequences in creating presuppositions about American foreign policy since then. Some of the points do specifically address the war effort, such as stating that the Allies are not in the war for their own aggrandizement. But other points are simply a utopian wish list.

Point six states in part: "All the men in all lands may live out their lives in freedom from fear and want."[128] And point eight speaks of disarmament and "abandonment of the use of force." That sounds good and would be nice, but it is a denial of reality to believe it will ever be that way. Evil exists in the world, and arms and force will always be necessary to restrain it. Human nature makes freedom from fear and want difficult as well. Although freedom is a natural desire, freedom by nature requires individual responsibility and accountability. That can be very frightening to people who have never experienced it. Human nature seeks freedom from fear and want in finding something to guarantee security and sustenance. That is the lie told by socialism and communism, leaders and government promising provision and security, which usually leads to tyranny. Another point of the Atlantic Charter emphasized that all nations should be self-determining in the government they wanted. However, in nations without a historical foundation in freedom, a large percentage of the population will often lean toward various isms that promise collective security.

The fatal presupposition the Atlantic Charter planted in American foreign policy is that the natural desire for freedom in men would lead them to desire American-style democracy. That, coupled with the success of post–World War II nation-building in Germany and Japan, led to attempts at nation-building throughout the world that have cost tens of thousands American lives, trillions of dollars, and met with very little success. American democracy requires a willingness to accept individual responsibility, accountability, and Judeo-Christian morality. If those qualities are absent in a culture, attempting to impose an American-style democracy are futile without a long-term commitment to provide security for generations to see the benefits of freedom. Even then, there is no guarantee nation-building will be successful, and the commitment necessary has usually been longer than the United States has been willing to give.

The current efforts of the United States in Iraq and Afghanistan demonstrate that America still suffers from this presupposition of a desire for American democracy and the same unwillingness to be committed long-term or lack of understanding of the commitment involved to have a chance at success. Consideration of the culture of a nation *must always* be paramount in the conception of realistic objectives.

Another idea that came to the fore in 1947 combined with the Atlantic Charter to have disastrous consequences for the American military over the next twenty-five years. That idea was the Truman Doctrine. Under fear of the spread of communism, the Truman Doctrine pledged the aid of the United States to any nation threatened by communism. By itself, the Truman Doctrine was a valid position for the United States to stand against communism. But combined with the presuppositions created by the Atlantic Charter, it led to unrealistic objectives in its implementation. The first consequences of these combined ideas began to be felt on July 5, 1950, south of Seoul, Korea.

On June 25, 1950, communist North Korean military forces rolled across the thirty-eighth parallel and attacked South Korea. The fledgling South Korean military was outnumbered and outgunned as they attempted to resist the communist onslaught. In the first week, the South Koreans lost half of their forces. Seoul was quickly overrun, and it became apparent that without US intervention, Korea would be unified under a communist government. In an effort that is symbolic of the poor decision making of the United States's involvement in Korea, two companies of the Twenty-Fourth Infantry Division were sent to aid the South Koreans in stopping the North. It was believed that the sight of American troops would encourage the South Koreans and frighten the North Koreans. The effort failed on both counts. Setting up about fifty miles south of Seoul on July 5, the two companies, designated Task Force Smith, attempted to stop the North Korean advance. They were quickly overwhelmed by enemy tanks and infantry. Colonel Smith, for whom the task force was named, and the survivors were able to break through the encircling communist forces and avoid complete annihilation, but they had suffered 185 casualties.[129] Tragically, and shamefully, many of the wounded were left behind to be captured by the North Koreans. Shamefully, not to the members of Task Force Smith who fought bravely, but shamefully that the United States was so naive and unprepared that wounded soldiers had to be left on an enemy field. By the time enough US forces reached Korea to halt the North's advance and establish the Pusan perimeter, 1,900 Americans lay dead and 900 had been taken prisoner.[130] Political ineptness and disregard for the elements that are necessary to prosecute war successfully cost American lives. Unfortunately, that disregard didn't end with the failure of Task Force Smith.

In the shadow of the great success of America in the Second World War, America had slashed defense spending drastically and shrunk the size of its military. Understandably, Americans and politicians were tired of war and hoped for a lasting peace. The public and government officials get a different type of combat fatigue than the soldier; it is a fatigue that just wants to forget about war and not deal with its reality. That usually leads to unpreparedness, and 1950 found the United States in that situation. Not only was the military smaller, but few of the divisions that did exist were combat ready. Training standards had slipped, and many troops were used to what was termed "soft" occupation duties in Japan and Europe. It all points to a lack of understanding that wars will happen and the nation needs to be constantly prepared.

President Truman, who had acted so courageously in his decision to drop the atomic bombs on Japan, seemed weary of that wartime decision-making responsibility as well. The commitment and determination to totally defeat the Axis powers gave way to a wish that the Korean problem could be solved with less than an all-out military effort. In fact, the war was often referred to as a police action, which some American troops found very offensive and insulting. Over fifty thousand Americans died during the three years of the Korean War. It was a brutal war, and the failure to treat it as such needlessly risked and wasted lives.

Unpreparedness isn't the only thing that plagued the United States throughout the Korean War. Of the six elements for a successful war policy that have been outlined, only one in the long term was held to by the United States that has eventually brought about the prosperous and democratic South Korea that exists today. The United States also missed the opportunity to act before a crisis. Korea is an artificially divided country. One of the unique things about Korea is that it is a homogeneous ethnic nation.[131] Often, nations and regions are divided along ethnic lines. And although at times, in Korea's long history, it was divided by warring factions, the Yi dynasty, which lasted roughly five hundred years, from 1400 to 1900, was generally a time of unification and cultural development that left its identifying mark on the nation. The

Treaty of Portsmouth that settled the war between Russia and Japan in 1905, brokered by Theodore Roosevelt, gave control of Korea to Japan. Emblematic of the times, the powerful ruled over the weak, and no one asked Korea what they wanted. In 1910, Japan annexed Korea as its own territory and remained in control of the nation until 1945. The Korean people suffered horribly under Japanese brutality. Men were conscripted into the Japanese military in their long war with China or used as slave labor. Women were taken to follow the army and used as sex slaves.

During World War II, the United States and Britain were forced by the exigencies of the time to deal with Soviet premier Stalin as a civilized human being instead of the brutal tyrant and sadistic murderer that he was. Stalin had agreed to get involved with the war against Japan after Germany was defeated. Britain and the United States hoped that the Soviet involvement would keep Japanese troops in Manchuria while the United States attacked the main Japanese islands. Without the development and use of the atomic bombs, the United States was facing the prospect of hundreds of thousands of casualties in a main-island invasion of Japan, and it is understandable that Soviet assistance would be desired. But the opportunistic Stalin simply wanted to wait while American troops gave their lives weakening Japan and then quickly move into northern Japan, Manchuria, and Korea to claim that territory.

After Japan's agreement to surrender, a hasty arrangement was reached to have the Japanese in southern Korea surrender to US forces while the northern forces would surrender to the Soviets. An arbitrary line of the thirty-eighth parallel was used to determine the division between north and south. Elections were to be held later that would unify Korea under one government. But the Soviets had other plans. Throughout the war, they had been preparing for the occupation of Korea and prepping their puppet dictator, Kim Il Sung. Needless to say, the North didn't participate in UN-held elections and set up their own communist government under Kim Il Sung.

Perhaps under the stress of Japan's sudden surrender and the need to occupy and establish civil governments in many nations around the world at the same time, the United States did the best it could for Korea in 1945. But having initiated the intervention in Korea, the United States abandoned South Korea in a few short years. By the summer of 1949, one year before North Korea attacked, US occupation troops had been withdrawn from South Korea. Around the same time, "U.S. Secretary of State Dean Acheson defined the limits of American interests in the Pacific at a line bordered by the Aleutians, Japan, and Okinawa."[132] Kim Il Sung interpreted these events that the United States wasn't interested in defending South Korea. With the approval of Joseph Stalin, Kim launched his attack on the South. It is possible the United States could have prevented the crisis of the Korean War had it just stayed engaged with South Korea and provided the necessary troops to maintain the security of a new nation. It was completely unrealistic to believe that a culture that went from dynasty to a thirty-five–year brutal occupation, to sudden liberation would be able to sustain itself as a new democracy. The American view of nation-building in Korea was to get a constitution in place and have an election, and the nation is built. As was said before and will be looked at later, it takes generations for cultures that haven't known freedom and democracy to become viable independent nations that can remain democratic. The quick withdrawal of America from South Korea in the late 1940s virtually sent an invitation to Kim Il Sung to attack and left a welcome mat for him. The United States missed its opportunity to act before a crisis.

The United States also failed to have clearly defined realistic objectives for the war once it became involved. President Truman feared the Korean conflict was the beginning of World War III. But faced with his doctrine to come to the aid of nations threatened with communist aggression, he felt compelled to take action. Working through the United Nations, a coalition was built to repel the communist North back across the thirty-eighth parallel. The bulk of the troops involved however were American. It took one month to halt the North Korean advance outside of Pusan. Fighting was bitter and heavy along the Pusan perimeter throughout the month of August 1950. As the North Koreans tried desperately to finish the conquest of the South, more and more US troops were landed at Pusan. In the meantime, General Douglas MacArthur, the supreme commander of the Allied Forces–Far East, had devised a plan to land the First Marine Division behind the North Korean forces at Inchon. On September 15, the Marines landed, and on the sixteenth the Eighth Army began its breakout from Pusan. By the end of September, what was left of the North Korean army was back across the thirty-eighth parallel. At that point, South Korea was liberated, and the UN objectives had been reached. The war could have ended then. The fighting had cost the United States around six thousand killed, a heavy price, but far less than the twenty-seven thousand more Korean battlefield deaths that would occur in the next thirty-four months of fighting.[133] And sadly, nothing was accomplished in those thirty-four months. The war ended in a shaky truce roughly along the same line as October 1, 1950, a shaky truce that exists today.

So what happened to continue the war? With the success that had occurred over the summer, some wanted to continue the war north and unify Korea. The problem was, it was an objective with restrictions. MacArthur was warned to halt any advance short of the Chinese border on the Yalu River. There were enough troops in Korea to finish off the North Korean army, but contingencies weren't made for the possibility of Chinese intervention. Perhaps MacArthur had become overconfident from victory. American forces were divided between the Eighth Army and X Corps, with separate commanders and no operational cooperation or means to support each other. Over the fall, the Chinese had begun to send troops across the Yalu. They remained hidden in the mountains, waiting for the right moment to commence their attack. Reports of skirmishes with Chinese were ignored or dismissed. At the end of November 1950, Chinese troops attacked the Americans in force. The Eighth Army in the west was driven back. The First Marine Division, ten thousand strong, on the west side of Chosin Reservoir was informed they were encircled by an estimated 120,000 Chinese. For approximately two weeks, from the end of November through the first half of December, the Marines fought their way through the Chinese a distance of over sixty miles back to the port city of Hungnam in temperatures that dipped twenty to thirty degrees below zero. They came back as Marines, bringing their dead, wounded, and equipment with them. One source lists casualties at almost 45 percent with 700 killed, 3,500 wounded, and 200 missing.[134] The Marine escape from the Chinese at Chosin is one of the great and heroic military feats in American history. The Chinese continued to push south and retook Seoul but were stopped south of the city. By the following spring, American forces had pushed the Chinese back north across the thirty-eighth parallel, and the fighting remained in that area for the rest of the war.

After the Chinese and North Koreans had been pushed out of the South the second time, efforts were initiated to end the war. But it continued for two years as negotiations were ongoing. The objectives became barren hills and scraps of land that could be used as bargaining chips in negotiations. MacArthur still wanted to win the war and take the fight to China if necessary, but whatever tact he may have possessed at one time was completely gone. His public statements and apparent unwillingness to work with the Truman administration resulted in him being relieved of command. So the war dragged on, and lives were lost because clear thought-out objectives were not expressed and held to at the start of the war. If the original objective of driving the North Koreans back across the thirty-eighth parallel would have been held to, the Chinese would not have gotten involved, the North Koreans would have been forced by circumstances to accept a truce, and the war would have ended in three months. Changing the objective to a halfhearted effort to unify all of Korea not only cost tens of thousands of American lives but hundreds of thousands more Korean and Chinese lives. The Chinese had warned through diplomatic channels that they would intervene if UN forces crossed the thirty-eighth parallel. The warnings were ignored or discounted. If the objective was really to unify Korea, then adequate numbers of troops and equipment needed to be committed to deal with the Chinese. Instead, brave American troops were sent ill equipped and outnumbered against an enemy that warned America they were coming. Failing to have clearly defined, realistic objectives costs lives.

America also failed to act decisively and prosecute the war aggressively. In the case of Korea, that failure was directly linked to failing to have clear objectives. After the initial shock of the North Korean attack was absorbed and halted, the first three months of the war were fought with determination and aggressiveness. The landing at Inchon, though risky, was a decisive use of force that pinched the North Korean supply lines and successfully destroyed much of the North's fighting ability. Those three months are a good example of how a clear objective and decisive and aggressive force work together to bring success. But the objective of unifying Korea *if* the Chinese didn't get involved was a disaster. The use of force was limited in an attempt not to encourage Chinese involvement. It is a deadly fallacy that weakness and appeasement prevent hostilities. Strength and show of force are what prevent war. Korea could have been unified, but it was predetermined that it would not be with the cost of a military conflict with China. Along with MacArthur's warning to stay away from the Yalu River, the border between China and Korea, other rules were in place that limited the use of force. When China was sending planes into North Korea, they would head back across the border if contact was made with US planes. The air force was ordered not to pursue them. Former Green Beret officer Gordon Cucullu spent many years on staff in Korea. He made the following statement: "Concepts of limited war, measured response, self-imposed restraint, undue fear of international opinion, deference to the UN, and enemy sanctuary areas were introduced during the Korean War. These concepts would haunt the military and the country for decades and persist to present day."[135]

A question still remains how much China would have been committed to keeping Korea from being unified. Initially, the Chinese troops that entered were not wearing Chinese uniforms. The Chinese government claimed the troops were just volunteers who wanted to help their Korean neighbors. That was a lie, but China tried to keep the names of the units involved and their officers a secret.

Usually, Chinese planes only engaged the air force and not American ground troops. It seems that China didn't want to risk an all-out war with the United States. It is usually forgotten that dictators don't have a first love for their country; their first love is always for themselves and staying in power. Their country is just a means to aggrandize themselves. A strongly reinforced initial invasion by the United States across the thirty-eighth parallel in October of 1950 may have caused Mao Zedong to think twice about sending his army into Korea, and if the initial attacks by the Chinese were repulsed by adequate US forces, self-preservation may have brought him to accept a unified Korea over risking his own position by insisting on war with the United States. What if scenarios are usually counterproductive, but this illustrates the point that the less-than-equipped and manned forces that did cross the thirty-eighth parallel in October of 1950, only encouraged China to believe they could succeed, and weak rules of engagement demonstrated China's presence was accepted on the battlefield. Indecisive and unaggressive action dictated by American policy cost American lives.

What did the United States get right in Korea? Thankfully, the element of perseverance was generally adhered to in the years post-armistice. Although South Korea was abandoned after World War II, the United States remained committed to defending and aiding South Korea after the conflict. Today, South Korea is a strong, free democratic nation with a robust economy and first-class military. The people of South Korea are profoundly thankful to the men and women who sacrificed so that they might have a chance at freedom. On May 6, 2013, on her visit to the United States, Korean president Park Geun-hye placed a wreath at the Tomb of the Unknown Soldier in Arlington National Cemetery. She said at the ceremony, "As the president of the Republic of Korea, I once again thank those who sacrificed themselves in the Korean War. Without them, Korea's prosperity would have been impossible."[136] But it was far from an easy road to get from war-torn country to prosperous democracy.

A brief look at the history of Korea since the armistice reveals the level of commitment and length of time that is necessary for successful nation-building. If there is one thing the United States can do to have clearer, realistic objectives in war, it would be to grasp the reality that nation-building is a generations-long process. Forty years is a good starting number to believe that troops, security, and aid will be required as an investment in a nation without a foundation in freedom or democracy. Much of that time is needed for the new government and people to learn to accept the rule of law.

Americans seem to forget how precious and essential that concept is. Acceptance of the rule of law is the foundation for a peaceful society. The written law must be the authority that citizens and government officials defer to. Without it, people begin to simply do what is right in their own eyes. Government leaders take action without a basis of authority. What recourse is there when people won't respect the law? At that point, the only option is force. Society becomes like a playground where one child says, "Stop, you can't do that!" and the other child responds, "Oh yeah! Make me!" The end result is a society that breaks down into anarchy, followed by authoritarian control. Peace and freedom have a fragile existence. At times, it is as if a whisper can shatter them. It is extremely dangerous when politicians play games that undermine respect for the rule of law. South Korea experienced these same growing pains.

The first president of South Korea was Syngman Rhee, a corrupt and at times ruthless authoritarian figure. He remained in power until 1960. In 1961, Park Chung-hee took over in a coup. He ruled until 1979, when he was assassinated. Another coup after his death brought Chun Doo-hwan to power. He was responsible for the brutal put-down of revolts in southwestern Korea. His time in power was characterized by almost constant protests. Finally in 1987, he stepped down and left his friend

Roh Tae-woo in power. Roh made a surprise move and called for free elections to be held. Thirty-four years after the 1953 armistice, Korea was beginning to make progress toward true democracy and respect for the rule of law.

Even though President Park was harsh on political opponents, ensuring his continual reelection, and limited freedom, he was instrumental in beginning to build a functioning economy. So little by little, from the armistice forward, Korea was making slow progress toward becoming the vibrant, healthy nation it is today. But it desperately needed the security and at times strong suggestions of the United States to continue on that path. Perseverance in nation-building was required! That rug of perseverance was almost pulled out from under South Korea by the inept US president Jimmy Carter.

Carter threatened and seemed determined to pull US troops out of South Korea. Not only did that shake American relations with Korea, but many pictured Kim Il Sung gleefully wringing his hands together waiting for the withdrawal to commence a new attack. The South Koreans began a frantic effort to start producing their own military equipment. That effort, though successful in the long term, pulled valuable resources away from other areas of economic growth. Thankfully, US military friends of Korea provided them with technical information on American weapons systems so the Koreans could reverse engineer and produce American-type weapons. The following statement by Gordon Cucullu reveals not only the feeling of many US officers at the time but a correct analysis of Carter's policy had it been carried out.

> Not surprisingly given the circumstances, most American officers were furious with the perceived indifference that the Carter administration showed to the South Koreans. Even more irritating was the knowledge that it would fall to the American military, whose advice Carter ignored, to clean up any mess he created. If there was a new shooting war the military would have to bleed and die to win it, not Jimmy Carter.[137]

The shortsightedness and ignorance of elected officials to the realities of the world are mind-boggling at times, and in the end, it is American soldiers that pay the price for that ignorance. Adherence to the six elements that comprise a successful war policy would go a long way to ensuring peace and saving lives. By the United States at least following one of those elements, perseverance, South Korea has become a friend, ally, and for her people, a free, thriving nation.

The lack of preparedness, ambiguous objectives, indecisive and unaggressive action that characterized the Korean War didn't just cost lives and prolong the war; it had long-term consequences for the morale of American troops. Morale and patriotic spirit are intangible factors in a fighting force that cannot be quantified and taught like military movements, tactics, and strategy; but they are nevertheless huge factors in the success of an army. Motivation and determination counterbalance a host of advantages the enemy may possess in personnel or arms. Because it is such an intangible factor, Clausewitz left its description at this: "History provides the strongest proof of the importance of moral factors and their often incredible effect."[138]

Returning veterans from the Korean War felt letdown and cheated by the policies that kept them from winning. Those who fought the last two years in the stalemate along the thirty-eighth parallel were falsely told in an attempt to boost morale that the war wasn't going to be won by occupying ground but by just killing the enemy.[139] Gordon Cucullu describes his father's sentiments upon returning from Korea this way.

> When the Korean War ended in an unsatisfactory armistice many of the veterans, including Dad, felt cheated and let down. After his relief and return to America, MacArthur had given his famous "no substitute for victory" speech. While it was derided as sentimental and outdated by the left, it rang true to the core with the veterans. Dying for a winning cause was unfortunate but necessary. One performed one's duty. Dying for a "limited war" with poorly understood objectives was uncomfortable. Dying while available weapons systems went unused and enemies had privileged sanctuaries was unacceptable.[140]

Gordon's father left the military.

Marine corporal Ron Burbridge expressed similar disappointment at the outcome of the war. Marines don't like to take ground twice. Given adequate troops and equipment, the unified Korean border would be at the Yalu River and all of Korea would be experiencing the prosperity that the South enjoys. But poor policy left the Marines no choice but to withdraw from Chosin, and twenty-four million North Koreans today live in fear, with the threat of starvation, imprisonment, torture, or death at the hands of a maniacal, dictatorial dynasty. Countless numbers have died in gulags and concentration camps. The tortures invented by the communists defy the imagination of civilized people. Former prisoner Soon Ok Lee said this: "The prison was a place where the "animals that do not have tails" lived. That is what the prisoners were. It is beyond human comprehension how the Communist Party could treat people this way."[141]

Corporal Burbridge is a member of the Frozen Chosin, the Marine Corps's appellation of the heroes of Chosin. Burbridge served with Second Platoon, Baker Company, First Battalion, Seventh Regiment, First Marine Division. He was part of the Inchon landings in September of 1950 that broke the back of the North Korean army and recaptured Seoul. On the way to Korea, Ron wondered why the Marines were getting involved in this faraway country. But when they were on Korean soil and saw the orphaned, starving children and the US POWs executed with their hands tied behind their backs, attitudes changed. It was good to stop such evil in Korea before it reached the United States.

In late November, west of Chosin, First Division commander general Oliver Smith told his men they were surrounded and withdrawing to Hungnam, but they would leave as Marines. Ron helped load the dead on trucks so that everyone got to go home. Ron credits much of his survival to Second Platoon's heroic leader, Lieutenant Lee, a Chinese American who on one occasion tricked a Chinese outpost that the Americans were actually a Chinese patrol so they could slip past. Hard fighting and uncommon valor typified the withdrawal from Chosin, along with a few miracles. Once, they were lost in blinding snow, but the clouds parted long enough to reveal the North Star in the frigid night sky. That was enough to get their bearings and continue on in the right direction. With shrapnel wounds and frostbite, Corporal Burbridge was on the last plane of wounded to leave Hagaru, and he remembered the sound of Chinese bullets hitting the plane. The rest of the division continued on, reaching Hungnam on December 11. Of the over two hundred men in Baker Company, only twenty-eight were able to walk into Hungnam.

Although there is disappointment over a war not finished, Ron is very proud of what South Korea has become and was sincerely touched by the gratitude of the South Korean people on his visit there. Ron is the typical heroic United States Marine and American serviceman. Having traveled across the world, Ron knows there is no country like America. Yet Ron doesn't think of himself as a hero; the real heroes, he says, were those that were loaded on the trucks, who didn't come back alive. The United States and Marine Corp flags proudly fly in front of Ron's house, and with Marine grit, he boldly asserts no one will ever take them down.[142] He won't be alone in defending those flags. A crowd of friends and neighbors will be standing right beside him. That is what makes America great. It is the proud citizens who love their country and serve to defend it. America has the best military in the world because of the quality of its citizens. Those soldiers want one thing first in war, to be allowed to win. America owes that to them. Politicians and the American public need to adhere to the elements of a successful war policy to make sure that happens. The rallying cry is, "No soldier will die in vain!"

In 1965, American troops were officially authorized to assume a combat role in the Republic of Vietnam, or as it is commonly referred to, South Vietnam. Instead of American policy makers learning from the mistakes in Korea, those mistakes were only accentuated in Vietnam. Vietnam displayed the mistakes of Korea on steroids, with tragic results.

The origins of the conflict in Vietnam were very similar to the origins of the conflict in Korea.[143] Both had their roots in decisions made at the conclusion of World War II. Like Korea, Vietnam—at the time part of pre–World

War II, French Indochina—was occupied by the Japanese. Communist Vietnamese independence fighters, led by Ho Chi Minh, fought the Japanese and their French colonial collaborators. Ho's guerrilla fighters received assistance from the United States in the way of training and arms, and they in return assisted and rescued US pilots shot down by the Japanese over Vietnam. In July 1945, Ho was very ill with malaria, and a US medic was brought in to treat him.

Ho's forces were able to wrest Hanoi from Japanese control in the late summer of 1945, shortly before the war ended. With the surrender of the Japanese to the Allies after the atomic bombs were dropped, Ho hoped to gain independence for Vietnam and recognition of a newly formed government under his leadership. He actively courted the support of the United States. But in direct conflict with the stated purposes in the Atlantic Charter to allow self-determination to liberated nations, the British moved into Saigon in Southern Vietnam to reestablish French rule over their former colony. Riots broke out in Saigon that were brutally put down by the British and French, who even enlisted the aid of Japanese troops that hadn't returned home yet. The United States, desirous to have the French as an ally in Western Europe, gave tacit approval and backed away from any support for an independent Vietnam. The decision of the United States to look the other direction as the British and French resumed the colonization of Vietnam left a lasting, negative impact upon the people. The French moved north from Saigon and took control of the cities, including Hanoi. A French response to a compromise offered by Ho was a naval bombardment of Haiphong that killed six thousand civilians.[144] Ho and his Viet Minh fighters retreated back into the mountains and continued their guerrilla war for Vietnamese independence.

The greatest failure of the United States in Vietnam was the failure to have a clearly defined, realistic objective. Goals were rarely clearly defined, but beyond that, they were never realistic given the history and culture of Vietnam. The precarious idea of nation-building becomes even more dubious when the culture of a nation is overlooked. The presupposition of self-determination leading to American democracy, coupled with the Truman Doctrine to halt communism led to a belief that democratic nations could be built even among unwilling populations. That is completely unrealistic, and again, it was American troops in Vietnam that paid the price for political ignorance of the basic elements to be successful in war.

The life of Ho Chi Minh is instructive to understanding a part of the Vietnamese mind-set that permeated the entire nation. That was a strong resentment of foreign intervention and a desire for independence. Ho Chi Minh was born in 1890 and, as a young man, took to work on a ship to see the world. He lived one year in New York and was living in Paris at the conclusion of World War I. At the armistice talks, he spoke out for Vietnamese independence but was ignored. Perhaps after living in New York, Paris, and London and experiencing the freedom enjoyed in the nations those cities belonged to, he expected support for an independent Vietnam. Instead of support for spreading the principles free nations were founded on, Ho saw the continuation of colonial rule and the oppression he had grown up with. Ho turned to the Communists as his hope for Vietnamese independence. After spending time with the Communist Party in France, Ho traveled to Moscow and received training under the Soviets.

Throughout the 1930s, he organized the Communist Party of Vietnam but was kept out of Vietnam by the French. He spent much of his time in the Soviet Union and China. The defeat of France by the Germans in 1940 and the resulting Japanese occupation of Vietnam provided Ho with the opportunity to return to Vietnam and begin his fight for independence. Despite his Communist training, Ho wrote, "It was patriotism and not Communism that originally inspired me."[145] It was that patriotic spirit that Ho was able to communicate to the people of Vietnam, who enabled his popular support. Most Vietnamese didn't have a proclivity for communism; they were willing to support any hope of independence.

The strong desire for independence within the nation of Vietnam was rooted in their history. Experiencing domination by the Chinese for one thousand years at one point and for lesser periods at other times, Vietnamese independence ended again in the mid-1800s. That was when the French decided to make Vietnam one of their colonies. The Vietnamese deeply resented the new French authorities, and resistance fighters instituted an almost continual guerrilla warfare against them. When the French returned after World War II, that fighting became more intense under the leadership of Ho Chi Minh. At first, Ho's Viet Minh struggled to gain outside support, but by 1949, Soviet and Chinese weapons started to flow to them while the French were aided by weapons and money from the United States. In 1954, the Viet Minh was strong enough to surround and assault a large French base at Dien Bien Phu. In a two-month siege, the Communists rained artillery rounds upon the French, who were cut off and could only be resupplied from the air. The French surrendered the position in May, and talks commenced in Geneva to end the conflict. A deal, called the Geneva Accords, between the French, Soviets, and Chinese divided Vietnam along the seventeenth parallel. The Communists under Ho Chi Minh would control the north, and the south would remain out of his control until an election could be held in 1956. The United States refused to sign the accords and backed a South Vietnamese government under the leadership of Ngo Dinh Diem. When it was time for the 1956 election to decide the fate of all of Vietnam, Diem and the United States refused the South's participation, setting up a permanently divided country on the seventeenth parallel. President Eisenhower commented that if the election would have been held, "Ho Chi Minh would have received 80% of the vote."[146] Apparently, self-determination was only allowed if the United States anticipated the outcome it wanted.

This began a futile attempt by the United States to prop up and build a democracy in South Vietnam. Although Ho Chi Minh tried to downplay his communist ideology in his early years seeking the aid of the United States, brutal property confiscations and executions took place in the midfifties that revealed his thorough indoctrination and utilization of communist methods, but the US-backed government in the South wasn't much better. From 1954 to the fall of South Vietnam in 1975, it was ruled by a string of corrupt men. Diem and his brother Nhu were killed in a coup in 1963 that had the blessing of the United States. In 1960, the Viet Cong emerged in the South with the aid of North Vietnam to bring about a unified Communist Vietnam. The United States continued to pour in increasing amounts of aid and military assistance to combat this threat. In some areas, there was outright support for the Viet Cong; in others, a complacency existed. To many, the United States was seen as another in a line of foreign powers supporting a government that was oppressing its people.

It is into this situation that American policy makers decided to officially authorize US troops for a combat role in 1965. Officially, because on an unofficial basis, American servicemen had been dying in Vietnam since the late 1950s. So US troops were sent to a country that resented foreign intervention, had a long desire to be independent and self-determining, had one hundred years experience fighting a guerrilla war against an occupier, and without the popular support of the citizens of the nation they would be fighting in.

The point in all this is not that Ho Chi Minh was a hero or that Communism is not evil or was the best thing for Vietnam; the point is the reality of the attitudes and culture of a people determine what *can*, *or cannot*, be accomplished in foreign policy. It was completely unrealistic for the Kennedy and Johnson administrations to believe that American-style democracy was possible in Vietnam through the measures of limited warfare they were engaging in. Even with a much larger scale invasion of North Vietnam and complete control of the country, generations of commitment, good will, and a just government would have had to be demonstrated to the Vietnamese people to even hope for a chance of success. Very few in America would have believed that was a proper course to take. Given the realities of Vietnam, a clearly defined, realistic objective would have been to walk away from an unwinnable situation right away. Instead, Vietnam ended in the same place fifty-seven thousand dead Americans later.

Along with the failure to have a clearly defined, realistic objective, America failed to act decisively or prosecute the war aggressively. Brigadier General Edwin Simmons, a Marine Vietnam veteran, said, "It's true we violated many of the basic principles of war. We had no clear objective. We had no unity of command. We never had the initiative. The most common phrase was 'reaction force'—we were reacting to them. Our forces were divided and diffused. Since we didn't have a clear objective, we had to measure our performance by statistics."[147]

First Cavalry Division commander Lieutenant General Harry Kinnard said this about the rules of engagement: "So you kept butting your head against the reality of a war where you have a fifty-yard line and you're told to play your game on one side of it. The other guy's able to play where you are, but you can't go where he is. At best that's a long-term stalemate, and our people aren't good at that."[148]

General Westmoreland, the commander in Vietnam, devised a strategy known as search and destroy. Apparently, the objective in Westmoreland's mind was to find all the Viet Cong and NVA in South Vietnam and kill them. The strategy was flawed at several points.

First and foremost, it was fighting the war on the enemy's terms and against the enemy's strength. Why let the enemy choose the terms of when and where the engagement takes place? And why face the enemy at his strongest point? Sun Tzu warned against such tactics millennia ago. It was a strategy that didn't respect the long history and experience of the Vietnamese in fighting a guerrilla war, and it was a strategy that failed to address the will of the North Vietnamese to continually send fresh troops south or the Viet Cong to raise new recruits. Almost no serious attempt was made to influence the North Vietnamese to stop fighting. Unbelievable quantities of bombs were dropped on North Vietnam, but the effect was similar to those dropped in World War II; it seemed to stiffen enemy resolve. No single industry was targeted that would have hindered the war effort by the

North. Many times vital targets were declared off limits: agriculture, fuel, ammo, power plants, factories. Like World War II, the advice to pick relatively few vital industries and concentrate on destroying them and preventing them from being rebuilt was ignored.

Despite the cultural environment in Vietnam, the absence of a clearly defined, realistic objective, and the halfhearted strategy that made the war unwinnable, the majority of American soldiers fought bravely and heroically. That was clearly displayed by the resounding victory won over the North Vietnamese and Viet Cong during the Tet Offensive.

Tet is the celebration of the Vietnamese lunar new year. The timing varies from year to year since it is based on the Gregorian calendar, but it falls between the end of January and first half of February. It is a high point in Vietnamese culture, with family gatherings and several days of celebration. During the Vietnam War, a truce was usually observed and leave was given to Vietnamese soldiers so they could spend the holiday with their families. In 1968, the Tet holiday began on January 31. The preceding summer, Communist officials from the North and South met in Hanoi to discuss plans for a large-scale offensive that was to be carried out during Tet. Attacks would be carried out simultaneously throughout South Vietnam.

During the summer and fall, arms and ammunition were carried south and staged for use during the offensive. Some NVA regulars would fight with the Viet Cong force of about sixty-seven thousand. Artillery and tank personnel were included in the strike forces with the hope they could capture and operate American equipment. In the northern part of South Vietnam, complete NVA divisions would carry out attacks against the Khe Sanh air base and the city of Hue. The entire plan was a departure from the normal guerrilla tactics of the North Vietnamese.

Another part of the operation was to take over radio stations throughout the South and broadcast a message from Ho Chi Minh in an attempt to create an uprising against the southern government and Americans. Some historians have compared the planning behind the Tet Offensive to the German execution and planning of the Battle of the Bulge in World War II.

In the months preceding the offensive, US intelligence was suspecting some type of operation by the Communists. General Westmoreland, listening to the advice of his subordinates, pulled some American troops back closer to Saigon and encouraged the South Vietnamese to cancel the Tet holiday leave. But his actions before the public created an impression that the war was going well. He had spent November of 1967 in Washington spouting optimism about the war.

When the Tet Offensive began, the public was shocked at the scale of the Communist attacks. Contrasted with Westmoreland's statements in the fall, it contributed to the suspicion of what was really happening in Vietnam compared with what the public was being told. Instead of making objective decisions about the war based on solid evidence, the Johnson administration seemed bent on securing South Vietnam and believing the war was winnable with the limited tactics that were being employed. That is the image they conveyed to the public as well, but with constant TV coverage and common sense, the American public was beginning to believe otherwise. The distrust that had been planted in the public by Johnson's administration had a negative influence on the reaction of the public to Tet.

In the early morning of January 30, Communists attacked seven cities north of Saigon. That night and through early the next morning on the January 31, cities were attacked up and down South Vietnam. Some of those cities were only defended by the South Vietnamese military. Often disparaged, many South Vietnamese units gave a good account of themselves, and others performed valiantly. Some of the most dramatic attacks occurred in Saigon. The US Embassy was assaulted, and some Viet Cong entered the compound through a hole blown in the wall. Although the embassy building itself was not breached, the visual picture of dead Viet Cong on the embassy grounds left a shocking impression on the public. Other sites around Saigon that were attacked included the American military headquarters at Tan Son Nhut Air Base, the Bien Hoa Air Base, and the Phu Tho Racetrack. The Cholon suburb in Saigon was occupied by Viet Cong for several days.

While the media in Saigon observing these events were shocked and terrified, the feeling among many in the military was one of satisfaction that the enemy, usually hidden and elusive, was finally out in the open, and the fight would now be advantage United States. One cavalry officer said on February 1:

> I can still remember the feeling of pride we had in our operations center the next morning when we heard the squadron commander's initial report…that Saigon, Bien Hoa, and Long Binh were literally ringed in steel… Five cavalry squadrons had moved through the previous day and night, converging on the Saigon area. When dawn broke, they formed and almost-continuos chain of more than five hundred fighting vehicles… We actually cheered…from that morning the outcome was never in doubt. We knew that our enemy could never match our mobility, flexibility, and firepower.[149]

Another soldier involved at the embassy called the action there "a piddling platoon action."[150] The action there lasted only six hours. The description as piddling is in the context of size and scope of operation. For the soldiers involved, every action is the most important and toughest fighting and every sacrifice deserves equal honor.

Farther north at Khe Sanh and Hue, the Marines experienced stiffer fighting against NVA regulars. At Khe

Sanh, six thousand Marine and South Vietnamese soldiers were surrounded by five divisions of the NVA. Though understrength, the NVA still may have numbered twenty thousand men. They remained around the base from January 20 to March 31, 1968. In an exhausting two and a half months, the Marines were hit by Communist artillery, mortar, and rocket attacks and had to keep a constant vigil against an all-out assault on the base. During the siege, the Marines were resupplied by air. The North Vietnamese paid a heavy price through US air attacks and withdrew as Operation Pegasus began to relieve Khe Sanh.

The city of Hue was an old imperial city filled with architecture reminiscent of Peking's Forbidden City and beautiful landscaping. Before the Tet Offensive, it was unmolested by the war; but on January 31, it was occupied by two regiments of NVA and VC allies. Vietnamese and separate American command compounds were surrounded but holding on within the city. Relief for the beleaguered compounds was slow in coming and understrength, but the platoons of Marines that were sent to the American compound acted with great courage and sacrifice and finally broke through. On the other side of the city, the ARVN (South Vietnamese, Army of the Republic of Vietnam) compound was reinforced by ARVN troops. Efforts to retake the city were slow. While other Communist units involved in the Tet Offensive were halted when it became apparent that the military objectives were not going to be achieved, the

NVA at Hue was told to hold the city. US command failed to understand the entrenchment and determination of the NVA and didn't send adequate forces to retake Hue. The Marines had to battle house by house through the city on the south side of the Perfume River to clear NVA while the ARVN worked to clear the north side. Casualties were extremely high. The First Cavalry fought hard outside the city to cut the NVA supply lines.

The efforts to retake the city were also hampered by the rules of engagement that were placed upon the Marines. An unwillingness to act decisively by American command cost Marine lives. Because of the historical nature of the city and its important architecture, artillery and air strikes against buildings were restricted. That meant the Marines had to clear every building room by room. Damage was still heavy throughout the city, but so was the cost in American lives. Who decided an old Vietnamese building was worth more than a marine life? It was the North Vietnamese who were using the buildings for cover and ambushes. If they wanted a historical Vietnamese city to be preserved, they could have let Hue remain an open city, but they didn't. Perhaps today's terrorists learned from Vietnam that America will grant sanctuary if schools, hospitals, important buildings, and family members are used as cover? And while the enemy is granted sanctuary and safe areas, Americans die.

When the Marines had the south side of Hue cleared, they went across the river to finish clearing for the ARVN.

The 1/5 Marines engaged the enemy on February 12. Nine days later, the first lieutenant of each of its ten rifle platoons was a casualty.[151] On February 24, Hue was back in American and ARVN hands, but the cost had been extremely high. The ARVN had 384 killed and 1,800 wounded; US Army, 74 killed and 507 wounded; and the Marines, 142 killed and 857 wounded. Estimates of enemy dead were over five thousand.[152]

When the Allied forces in World War II sent the Germans back through the Ardennes after the Battle of the Bulge, it was declared a victory for the Allies and defeat for the Germans. Germany lost manpower and equipment that it couldn't replace and wouldn't be available to take up defensive positions against the Allied advance into Germany. By the beginning of March 1968, the last remnants of the Tet Offensive were being cleaned up. Communist losses were over forty thousand dead. The Viet Cong were eliminated as a fighting force. The enemy had presented himself, and the American military had swiftly and heroically driven him back into hiding. Wounded Marines had limped along beside their comrades to finish clearing Hue. America had demonstrated the character and fighting spirit of its young men once again. But instead of being celebrated as a victory, the Tet Offensive was perceived as a defeat. After repeatedly being told the war was going well by the Johnson administration, the American public was shocked that the Communists could even mount such a large-scale offensive.

What the Tet Offensive did accomplish was reveal the fallacies of the premises upon which the United States was engaging the war. After Tet, it was clear Westmoreland's policy of attrition was not working. Unrealistic objectives, limited engagement, indecisive action, and an unwillingness to prosecute the war aggressively on North Vietnamese soil were not going to bring about victory.

The influential Walter Cronkite visited South Vietnam and the city of Hue while the fighting was still ongoing in February 1968. On February 27, he told the American public his perspective on what he saw and the war.

> We have been too often disappointed by the optimism of the American leaders… To say that we are closer to victory today is to believe, in the face of the evidence, the optimists who have been wrong in the past… To say that we are mired in stalemate seems the only realistic, yet unsatisfactory, conclusion…it is increasingly clear to this reporter that the only rational way out will be to negotiate, not as victors, but as an honorable people who lived up to their pledge to defend democracy, and did the best they could.[153]

How sad to say, "Negotiate, not as victors." Vietnam cast a shadow of doubt on the American military, which it should not have. Vietnam cast a shadow of doubt to our ally Korea, and the rest of the world about American commitment. That doubt was rightly deserved. Vietnam revealed that American political decision making about war was mired in fantasy. A disregard for the elements necessary for a successful war policy had once again lost American lives. How sad that Vietnam ended where it would have if America hadn't gotten involved at all. All the blood, sweat, sacrifice, and effort seems lost in a vain cause. But Vietnam veterans can be proud of the service they gave to America. Though the politicians didn't understand what they were doing, America's soldiers served and died for each other. They represented America. And they did it well.

Is it wishful thinking to believe that the politicians who send America's troops to war will ever understand what war is and what it takes to win? There was a glimmer of hope after the terrorist attacks on September 11, 2001. In President George W. Bush's comments throughout the remaining month that year, he spoke of the equal culpability those who harbored or aided terrorists shared with the terrorists. On the evening of September 11, he said, "We will make no distinction between the terrorists who committed these acts and those who harbor them." Later, before Congress, he said, "Either you are with us, or you are with the terrorists."[154] President Bush was one of the greatest wartime presidents America has ever had. His deep love for the country and care for its troops was evident in both his words and actions. But the powerful words he spoke that September didn't filter down to the rules of engagement for the soldier on the field. Perhaps a symptom of an entrenched bureaucracy that believes kindness will win over the enemy.

In The National Security Strategy of the United States of America dated September 2002, several positive statements were made that revealed an effort to fight war differently. A significant argument was made explaining the need to act before a terrorist attack. An effort was made to define who the enemy was, and a comment was placed in the document calling for realism in goals. "The United States should be realistic about its ability to help those who are unwilling or unready to help themselves."[155] But already, the president's comments a year earlier were being watered down by bureaucrats even though the president repeated his remarks in the introduction to the strategy paper. The president stated in his introduction: "And America will hold to account nations that are compromised by terror, including those who harbor terrorists—because the allies of terror are the enemies of civilization."[156] But the paper itself leaves this comment regarding policy: "…denying further sponsorship, support, and sanctuary to terrorists by convincing or compelling states to accept their sovereign responsibilities."[157] While President Bush was very clear: the official policy was watered down to be almost unintelligible, convincing, compelling, sovereign responsibilities: all words that leave to much room for a diplomatic waste of time. A clearer and better statement would have been, "America will kill the terrorists and those who aid them." Sadly, the failure of the president's statements and views to be implemented on the battlefield cost American lives.

Mullah Ahmad Shah was carrying out attacks on US forces along the Pakistani and Afghan border throughout the first half of 2005. His group, the Bara bin Malek Front, was associated with the Taliban. After an attack in early June 2005 that left three Marines dead, he became a high priority target for coalition forces. He was known to move among the villages in the Hindu Kush Mountains of Kunar Province in northeast Afghanistan. The terrain is extremely rugged and inhabited by the Pashtun people.

The Pashtuns are an ancient ethnic group with a proud heritage of controlling the mountainous regions where they live in Afghanistan and Pakistan. They comprise about 40 percent of the population of Afghanistan, numbering 12.5 million, while twenty-eight million live in Pakistan.[158] Some of the Pashtuns and their villages were cooperative with the United States, but many in the region supported the Taliban. Shah drew fighters from the sympathetic villages and was protected and supplied by them. The support of the villagers, with their knowledge of the terrain and agility in the mountains, made Shah a difficult target to capture.

A plan was put in place in June 2005, named Operation Red Wings, to capture or kill Shah. Twice during the month, the operation was scheduled and then aborted as intelligence believed Shah had changed his location. Finally, on the night of June 27, four Navy SEALs were dropped on a reconnaissance mission, which was the first phase of Red Wings. They were Lieutenant Michael Murphy, Petty Officer Second Class Matthew Axelson, Petty Officer Second Class Danny Dietz, and Lead Petty Officer Marcus Luttrell. The events that followed the beginning of Operation Red Wings have gained national attention through the bestselling book *Lone Survivor* and movie by the same title.

The SEAL's mission was to take up position high above the village Shah was suspected to be at the time and confirm his presence there. Once the target was confirmed, an assault force would be brought in to surround his camp and neutralize him; other forces would follow up with a sweep through the valley to clear any of his remaining fighters. The entire operation was scheduled to take several days. The first night was rough for the four SEALs as cold rain and treacherous landscape made climbing difficult and dangerous. It took the supremely fit men seven hours to make the four-mile trek into position. After some repositioning at the sight to get a clear view of the village, the four settled in to watch and wait.

It is rare that the impact of political decisions, made halfway around the world, upon the lives of men and women in uniform are made so personal to so many people. But the popularity of the *Lone Survivor* book and movie have made the story of what happened to Marcus Luttrell and the other SEALs on that remote mountain side in Afghanistan personal and real. It has revealed the terrible price service members have to pay for political ignorance, or denial, of the reality of war. To prosecute war aggressively, a key element in a successful war policy means to clearly define who the enemy is. President Bush repeatedly stated that those who harbor or aid terrorists would be treated as terrorists. A correct and aggressive view. But the rules of engagement on the field in Afghanistan that June were much different.

The four SEALs on recon were stumbled upon by three Afghan goat herders late in the morning on the twenty-eighth. Their position being compromised, a decision needed to be made about what to do next. According to the rules of engagement, "If the compromise was by known anticoalition militia (ACM), they were to be neutralized. If the compromise was by civilians, they were to be turned loose and moved to a new location."[159] In general, the rule of engagement regarding use of force that day was: "We may not open fire until we are fired upon or have positively identified our enemy and have proof of his intentions."[160]

In the attempts to interrogate the three herders, they would not reveal any information about the Taliban or who may have been in the village. But their posture and looks revealed they were filled with hate for the SEALs and they were aiding the Taliban by their silence. If released, they would betray the SEAL's position to Shah or whoever was in the village. In the ensuing discussion by the four team members, two options emerged: kill the herders to make an escape or release them and hope for the best. To kill them and break the rules of engagement meant risking being charged with murder.

Earlier in Lieutenant Murphy's career, he attended junior officer training course. Admiral Olson was addressing the class and discussing the consequences of the objectives the military was given in Mogadishu, Somalia, in 1993. Someone asked what the mission should have been. In his brief statement about what might have been different, he made this conclusion: "But these are big issues, well above your pay grade and mine. Let's talk about things we can do—what you can do as future naval leaders as you train and prepare your platoons for special operations."[161] Admiral Olson was rightly reinforcing to the young officers the important American principle of civilian rule of the military. Like the rule of law, civilian control of the military is one of those frail threads that needs to be honored for a free society to exist. Most Americans take it for granted that the military will obey the civil authority, nothing but respect for the principle ensures it. Eventually, on the side of that mountain in Afghanistan, nineteen US servicemen sacrificed their lives to honor that principle and obey the rules of engagement they were given.

But that question of what should the mission have been is *not* above the pay grade of every American citizen. In fact, it is the duty of every citizen to understand the elements necessary for a successful war policy, *demand* that politicians adhere to them, and thereby give American soldiers the best opportunity to succeed and come home alive.

America was attacked on September 11, 2001, by al-Qaeda members whose leadership was being harbored by the Taliban in Afghanistan. That is why American forces were in Afghanistan. Every citizen of Afghanistan, fair or not, needed to make a choice whose side they would be on, but it was a choice forced upon them by the actions of their own government. Those villages that cooperated with America received aid and assistance. Those villages that aided the Taliban needed to know the harsh consequences of their choice. The three herders that stumbled upon Mike Murphy, Matt Axelson, Danny Dietz, and Marcus Luttrell held their fate in their own hands. Ideally, they could have cooperated and given valuable intelligence to the SEALs, spared their lives, and saved many American lives by bringing about the death of Shah. *Their* choice to refuse to cooperate made them aids to terrorists and should have resulted in their death to preserve American life. How many lives were lost by not prosecuting the war aggressively? Nineteen Americans that day. It has been stated before that the civilian population supporting the enemy needs to be made to feel hopeless in that effort. That requires kindness for cooperation with America but consequences for enemy support. Marcus Luttrell put it this way: "Because in the end, your enemy must ultimately fear you, understand your supremacy."[162] That is the reality of war, and the reality of the enemy faced in terrorism. There can be no compromise. "No one can hate quite like a terrorist. Until you've encountered one of these guys, you don't understand the meaning of the word *hate*."[163]

As the goat herders bounded away, the team set out to find a better defensive position and hope for dark to escape. But an hour and a half later, up to one hundred heavily armed Taliban fighters were closing in on them. The fighting was ferocious. Shah's fighters were led well. They kept pressure up on the team's flanks, making the only avenue of escape jumping down the mountainside. The SEALs took a beating as they rolled uncontrollably down the steep sides, losing most of their equipment along the way. It didn't take long before they were all seriously wounded. Danny Dietz, Matthew Axelson, and Marcus Luttrell each received the Navy Cross for their actions that day, June 28, 2005. Michael Murphy received the Congressional Medal of Honor, America's highest award.

So what did the consequences of letting the goat herders, Taliban informants, go look like? Danny died first. Shot multiple times, once through the neck and unable to speak, he was being pulled along by Marcus, still firing his weapon to cover their retreat, when a final slug caught him in the face. Axe, as his friends called him, among his other wounds, suffered a horrible shot to the head. But he kept fighting. After a RPG blew Marcus off a ledge, separating him from Axe, Axe still kept going. They had trouble finding his body because he covered one hundred yards or more from the last position Marcus had seen him. Then there was Lieutenant Murphy. The team had been unable to get communication with base during the firefight. With ammo running low and the grievous wounds he suffered, including a new chest wound for Mike, he got out his phone and started walking out into the open to get a signal. Sitting on a rock, exposed, and bullets flying around, he finally got through to base and requested help. While he was talking, a bullet hit him in the back and blew out through the front of his chest. He went to his knees and dropped his phone and gun. After a brief pause, he picked the phone back up and said, "Roger that, sir. Thank you."[164] Then he got up, took his rifle, and found a position to continue firing until his body quit.

The Taliban lost Marcus after the RPG hit, and he went over the ledge. Waiting for cover of darkness, he began to try and make his way out. His left leg was full of shrapnel, three vertebrae were cracked in his back from the terrible falls, as well as a shoulder injured. The falls had also broken his nose, gashed his forehead, and scraped one side of his face completely. Some of the Taliban searching for him the next day caught a glimpse of him and put a bullet through the damaged left leg. Literally dying of thirst from lack of water and loss of blood, he was found by some sympathetic villagers who took him and gave him aid. According to Pashtun custom, they offered to Marcus *lokhay warkawal*, which meant that they would not only take care of him but they also vow to defend and protect him to death. Throughout the days he was in the village, they risked their lives to protect Marcus from the Taliban. Finally on July 3, Marcus was rescued by a team of rangers and Green Berets.

Unknown to Marcus on the day of the battle, a rescue force had set out to find the embattled SEALs after Mike's heroic call. But as one team was preparing to rope down from the helicopter, an RPG hit, knocking it from the sky. There were sixteen on board, eight Navy SEALs and eight Night Stalkers of the 160th Special Operations Aviation Regiment, no one survived. All because of three goat herders who informed for the Taliban. They were just as guilty for the death of those men as if they had pulled the trigger themselves.

The unbelievable courage displayed by the members of SEAL Team 10 on the mountainside of Afghanistan and of the men who lost their lives trying to rescue them is typical of America's soldiers and Special Forces. Special Forces training isn't about finding men with the bodies of Superman; in fact, the minimum physical entry requirements for SEALs training are not that difficult. The training itself produces the extreme conditioning, if the trainees body can withstand the rigors. What Special Forces training does is separate those who will quit from those who will succeed or die trying.

Mike Murphy demonstrated this long before Afghanistan. During Hell Week of BUD/S training, Mike developed cellulitis from the prolonged exposure to the ocean water. He was able to keep it hidden from the medics for a while. By the time a roommate got help, Mike's feet were black on bottom and between his toes. He spent several days in the hospital on powerful antibiotics in a successful effort to save his feet from amputation.[165] He is not alone in that determination. Nor is it reserved only for the Special Forces, as evidenced by the heroic actions of seemingly "normal" service members in the face of extreme danger. It typifies the American soldier throughout history. Their courage and dedication deserve better than rules of engagement that jeopardize their lives for the sake of the enemy and cause their greatest fear to be being prosecuted by their own nation.

The Taliban could not exist without the aid of the villages they frequent. To hold those villages that support the Taliban guiltless and fail to create negative consequences for their actions does nothing to bring about victory over the Taliban and security for the struggling Afghan government. Prosecuting war aggressively means defining the enemy accurately and treating them as enemies. Failing to do so only ends up prolonging war and costing lives. The Taliban never directly attacked the village that was protecting Marcus for fear of angering the Pashtuns who were supporting them. Marcus described the Taliban dependence on the villages this way:

> This armed gang of tribesmen, who were hell-bent on driving out the Americans and the government, could not function up here in these protective mountains entirely alone. Without local support their primitive supply line would perish, and they would rapidly begin to lose recruits. Armies need food, cover, and

cooperation, and the Taliban could only indulge in so much bullying before these powerful village leaders decided they preferred the company of the Americans.[166]

Including the villages that support the Taliban in the list of enemies is essential to drying up that support the Taliban enjoys. That doesn't mean wiping out whole villages with no military objective; that has already been shown to be counterproductive. But it does mean creating real consequences for supporting the enemy. From vulnerability to air strikes for hiding Taliban fighters or weapons, to killing a few goat herder informants, the choice that day wasn't just between the four lives of the SEAL Team 10 members or the three goat herders. Perhaps if it was, then the noble thing to do would be to let them go. As employees of the United States of America, for the purpose of securing the life and liberty of all Americans and those engaged on a foreign field of battle, the choice, or perhaps better, the question, was, how many will die if these three herders aren't killed? That day, it was nineteen more.

Epilogue

War is horrible by its nature. There isn't any way around it. It is difficult to have the resolve as a nation to do what needs to be done to win. It may seem like an oxymoron to say that the way to peace and saving lives is through aggressiveness on the battlefield. But it is true because of man's human nature. Victory is the submission of one side to the will of the other. If that is the goal, then the key determining factor in how that is accomplished must be based upon the nature of man, based on what causes men to submit. This book is an examination of those elements necessary for a successful war policy, successful defined as saving American lives, reducing enemy casualties, and bringing about victory. Those elements are derived from the fact that wars will happen, the nature of war, and human nature. All are critical and work together to reduce the frequency of wars and shorten their length, thereby saving precious lives. To be successful in war, a nation must

- Be prepared
- Act before a crisis

- Clearly define realistic objectives
- Act decisively
- Prosecute war aggressively
- Persevere

It is crucial and imperative that citizens be involved in driving the politics behind America's war policy. While some may assume that is the realm of military planners and thinkers, quite the opposite is true. The American military is rightly under civilian rule. The military cannot make the decisions concerning: funding for preparedness, when to use force, what the objective of military action should be, how much force to use, who is the enemy, and continuing the effort. Those are decisions the military waits to be instructed on by the civilian government leadership. And who is the government in America? "We the people." So it is definitely within the "pay grade" of the American people to understand the nature of war and what elements are necessary for war to be successful. For too long, too many citizens have left these decisions for elected politicians to make without pressure from their constituents. The results and costs have been horrific in the lives that have been lost in vain—soldiers dying as a result of policies that were doomed to failure before they were even begun.

Who will watch out for America's soldiers? They are the most loyal, dedicated, patriotic, trained, efficient, and effective fighting force in the world. But they are waiting on us, the citizens, to tell them how, when, and where they will be used. Like the members of SEAL Team 10, they will obey their directives even when the foolishness of them is obvious, and the results, deadly. No more. It's time for the citizens of America to say no more will her sons and daughters be the pawns of a misguided political establishment that doesn't have the foresight to see the reality of this evil world or the courage to act within the best interests of America.

Not all the blindness about war, its reality, the world we live in, or the harshness required to stop evil is based on wishful utopian dreams that the world isn't as evil as it appears. Much of the hesitancy to prosecute war as it needs to be prosecuted exists because America truly is a moral nation. Its Judeo-Christian heritage has instilled a disdain and distaste for the brutality of war. It goes against the compassionate nature of Americans to execute the aggressiveness that wins war. How does a Christian reconcile their beliefs in the love, compassion, and charity of Christ for man with the brutality necessary to restrain man through war? It does not make supporting war easy, which is a good thing, but that reconciliation comes from recognizing that government is not a person. Government is an institution ordained by God for the very purpose of being a restraint on evil so that man might live in peace. The duty of a Christian to act in love, compassion, charity, and at times turn the other cheek toward fellow man is not in conflict with the duty of a Christian citizen to support and participate in the fulfillment of government's duty to secure the rights of its citizens and defend against evil. That compassionate nature compels Americans to want to end war quickly. But that only comes about, in a lasting way, when war is prosecuted aggressively. One day, in Jesus Christ's kingdom, there will be no war. But that day is not yet.

President Lincoln knew what it was like to be locked in that awful conflict of wanting the horror of war to end but knowing it couldn't yet. He bore the responsibility of pushing the Union generals forward to finish the conflict despite the gruesome butcher's bill those orders created. When tempted to quit, when tempted to pull back from what was necessary to finish the job, he remembered the men who had done their part, those who had given their lives to carry the cause forward. Perhaps he could see them looking behind them from the field where they had fallen, handing the battle flag on to the next soldier to carry it to the enemy's heights. It was, and is, for them that we must continue on. That we must give our soldiers what they need, and the rules they need, to bring about victory. That we must resolve "that these dead shall not have died in vain."

Notes

1. The narrative of President Lincoln's thoughts is fictional, but it is based on historical facts about his character, actions surrounding the Battle of Gettysburg, and events of the days before and after the Gettysburg Address. Sources specifically used include the following:

    Stephen B. Oates, *With Malice toward None: A Life of Abraham Lincoln* (NewYork: HarperPerennial, 1994).

    Rich Lowry, *Lincoln Unbound: How an Ambitious Young Railsplitter Saved the American Dream—and How We Can Do It Again* (New York: HarperCollins, 2013).

    T. J. Stiles, ed., *In Their Own Words: Civil War Commanders* (New York: Perigee, 1995).

    Michael Shaara, *The Killer Angels* (New York: Ballantine Books, 1996).

Abraham Lincoln Research Site, "Abraham Lincoln's Invitation to Speak at Gettysburg and the Meaning of the Gettysburg Address," accessed December 8, 2014, www.rogerjnorton.com/Lincoln58.html.

LaFantasie, Glenn. "Lincoln and the Gettysburg Awakening." *Journal of the Abraham Lincoln Association*, accessed December 10, 2014, www.quod.lib.umich.edu/j/jala/2629860.0016.108/—lincoln-and-the-gettysburg-awakening?rgn=main;view=fulltext;ql=gettysburg.

2. Oats, *With Malice toward None*, 340.
3. Stone Sentinels, "Battle of Gettysburg Facts," accessed November 24, 2014, www.gettysburg.stonesentinels.com/Gettysburg_Facts/Gettysburg_Facts.php.
4. Dick Camp, "3/5 'Darkhorse' Clears City." *Leatherneck* 97, 12 (2014), accessed December 15, 2014, www.mca-marines.org/leatherneck/2014/12/35-darkhorse-clears-city.
5. Susan Murphy, "10 Years After Battle For Fallujah, Marines Reflect On 'Iconic Fight'." *npr.org*, November 7, 2014. www.npr.org/2014/11/07/362156306/10-years-after-battle-for-fallujah-marines-reflect-on-iconic-fight (accessed December 15, 2014).
6. Jim Michaels, "Al-Qaeda militants in Iraq seize Fallujah," *USA Today*, January 4, 2014, accessed

December 15, 2014, www.usatoday.com/story/news/world/2014/01/04/al-qaeda-iraq-fallujah-ramadi/4317125/.
7. "IS: More Extreme than the Extremists," *The Voice of the Martyrs* (November 2014): 6–7.
8. "10 Years after Battle For Fallujah, Marines Reflect On 'Iconic Fight'," *npr.org.*
9. "3/5 'Darkhorse' Clears City." *Leatherneck.*
10. *The New York Times on the Web*, Learning Network accessed December 22, 2014, www.nytimes.com/learning/general/onthisday/bday/0803.html. April 19, 1945, "Ernie Pyle Is Killed on Ie Island; Foe Fired When All Seemed Safe."
11. Ibid.
12. C. L. Sulzberger, David G. McCullough, ed., *The American Heritage Picture History of World War II* (American Heritage Publishing, 1966), 400.
13. Ibid., 349.
14. John 15:13. *New King James Version.*
15. *Voices of Democracy*, The US Oratory Project, "Edward Everett, 'Gettysburg Address' (19 November 1863)," accessed December 18, 2014, http://voicesofdemocracy.umd.edu/everett-gettysburg-address-speech-text/.
16. Ralph Happel, "Major John Pelham—Arms and the Boy: The Great Cannoneer; Killed at 24, Was One of the War's Most Glamorous Figures," *Richmond*

Times-Dispatch, March 26, 1939, Then And Now Richmond, accessed December 23, 2014, www.richmondthenandnow.com/Newspaper-Articles/John-Pelham.html.

17. Dr. J. W. Jones, *Life & Letters of Gen. Robert Edward Lee* (Neale, 1906; reprint ed., Harrisonburg: Sprinkle, 1986), 209.
18. Ibid., 377.
19. Ibid., 209.
20. Robert Lewis Dabney, *Life and Campaigns of Lieutenant General Thomas J. Stonewall Jackson* (Boston: Scrymgeour, Whitcomb & Co., 1865; reprint ed., Harrisonburg: Sprinkle, 1983), 207.
21. Ibid., 160.
22. *In Their Own Words*, 63.
23. *With Malice toward None*, 323.
24. Ibid., 324.
25. *Life and Campaigns*, 619.
26. *Life & Letters*, 209.
27. *Life and Campaigns*, 627.
28. Ibid., 625.
29. *Life & Letters*, 208.
30. Ibid., 436–473.
31. Ibid., 259.
32. Ibid., 35.
33. Ibid., 378.
34. Ibid., 379.

35. Ibid., 482.
36. Ibid., 127.
37. Ibid., 82, 83.
38. Ibid., 119.
39. Ibid., 120–121.
40. Ibid., 122.
41. Ibid., 133.
42. *Life and Campaigns*, ix.
43. Ibid., 125–126.
44. "Edward Everett, 'Gettysburg Address' (19 November 1863)," paragraph 12.
45. *Life and Campaigns*, 174.
46. "Edward Everett, 'Gettysburg Address' (19 November 1863)," paragraph 43.
47. Gary Wills, ed., *The Federalist Papers* (New York: Bantam Books, 1982) 32.
48. Ibid., 62.
49. Ibid., 70–72.
50. *Lincoln Unbound*, 128.
51. *With Malice toward None*, 143.
52. Ibid., 232.
53. Ibid., 316.
54. Niccoló Machiavelli, *The Prince* (Mineola: Dover, 1992) 21.
55. Most of this information is taken from Marie von Clausewitz's preface to the 1832 publication of *On War*.

56. Michael Howard and Peter Paret, ed. and trans., Carl Von Clausewitz, *On War* (Princeton: Princeton University Press, 1976), 61.
57. Ibid.
58. Ibid., 75.
59. Ibid., 87.
60. Ibid., 76.
61. D. E. Tarver, ed. and trans., *The Art of War* (Lincoln: iUniverse, 2002), 69.
62. Ibid., 70.
63. Frederic Bastiat, *The Law* (Irvington-on-Hudson: Foundation for Economic Education, 1998), 1.
64. *The Prince*, 69.
65. *On War*, 128.
66. Ibid., 220.
67. Ibid., 137.
68. *The American Heritage Picture History of World War II*, 134.
69. *The Prince*, 37–38.
70. Sherry Sontag and Christopher Drew, *Blind Man's Bluff* (New York: Public Affairs, 1998), 259.
71. Ibid., 158–183.
72. Ibid., 275.
73. Ibid., 270.
74. Erik Slavin, "Amid US plans for continued Asia presence, a shrinking submarine fleet." *Stars and Stripes*, August 22, 2014, accessed January 21,

2015, www.stripes.com/news/amid-us-plans-for-continued-asia-presence-a-shrinking-submarine-fleet-1.299433.
75. Robert Farley, "US Navy Orders 10 Virginia-class Submarines at a Record Cost of $17.6 Billion." *The Diplomat*, May 3, 2014, accessed January 21, 2015, www.thediplomat.com/2014/05/us-navy-orders-10-virginia-class-submarines-at-a-record-cost-of-17-6-billion/
76. *The Prince*, 6.
77. Donald Sommerville, *World War II: Day by Day* (Greenwich: Dorset Press, 1989), 10–14.
78. World Nuclear Association, "Nuclear Power in Iran," accessed January 24, 2015, www.world-nuclear.org/info/Country-Profiles/Countries-G-N/Iran/
79. Jessica Elgot, "Iran's President Mahmoud Ahmadinejad: His Most Outrageous Quotes On 9/11, Israel And The Holocaust." *The Huffington Post UK*, June 14, 2013, accessed January 23, 2015, www.huffingtonpost.co.uk/2013/06/13/irans-president-mahmoud-a_n_3434408.html
80. Abbas Milani, "The Green Movement." *The Iran Primer, United States Institute of Peace*, accessed January 23, 2015, http://iranprimer.usip.org/resource/green-movement
81. *On War*, 579.

82. Dr. Richard W. Stewart, "The United States Army in Somalia, 1992–1994." United States Forces, Somalia After Action Report and Historical Overview, www.history.army.mil/html/documents/somalia/SomaliaAAR.pdf (accessed January 25, 2015).
83. *On War*, 69.
84. *The Prince*, 47–48.
85. Ali Khedery, "Why we stuck with Maliki—and lost Iraq" *The Washington Post*, July 3, 2014, accessed January 26, 2015, www.washingtonpost.com/opinions/why-we-stuck-with-maliki—and-lost-iraq/2014/07/03/0dd6a8a4-f7ec-11e3-a606-946fd632f9f1_story.html
86. Ibid.
87. *The Art of War*, 10.
88. *On War*, 204.
89. Ibid., 75.
90. *The Art of War*, 10.
91. Frontline, "Ambush in Mogadishu, Chronology: The US/UN In Somalia," accessed January 28, 2015. www.pbs.org/wgbh/pages/frontline/shows/ambush/etc/cron.html.
92. William Booth, "Here's what really happened in the Gaza war (according to the Israelis)." *The Washington Post*, September 3, 2014, accessed January 28, 2015, www.washingtonpost.com/blogs/worldviews/

wp/2014/09/03/heres-what-really-happened-in-the-gaza-war-according-to-the-israelis/
93. Isabel Kershner, "Israeli Government Watchdog Investigates Military's Conduct in Gaza War." *The New York Times*, January 20, 2015, accessed January 28, 2015, www.nytimes.com/2015/01/21/world/middleeast/israel-hamas-gaza-strip-war-investigation.html?_r=0
94. *The Prince*, 2.
95. *Life and Campaigns*, 134.
96. *On War*, 87.
97. *Life & Letters*, 206.
98. *On War*, 259.
99. *With Malice toward None*, 402.
100. *Life and Campaigns*, ix.
101. *On War*, 259.
102. Ibid., 643.
103. Nathan D. Jensen, "Battle of the Berezina," accessed January 30, 2015, www.arcdetriomphe.info/battles/berezina/
104. *On War*, 193.
105. *With Malice toward None*, 396.
106. *Life & Letters*, 439.
107. National Churchill Museum, National Churchill Museum Blog, "Those Who Fail to Learn from History... November 16, 2012," accessed February

3, 2015. www.nationalchurchillmuseum.org/blog/churchill-quote-history/.
108. *The American Heritage Picture History of World War II*, 307.
109. *Life & Letters*, 353.
110. *The Prince*, 23.
111. Albert Speer, *Inside the Third Reich* (New York: Touchstone, 1970), 230.
112. Ibid., 31.
113. Ibid., 344.
114. Ibid., 281–282.
115. Ibid., 286.
116. Ibid., 352.
117. John Hersey, *Hiroshima* (New York: Vintage, 1989), 67.
118. Maurice Isserman, *America at War: World War II* (New York: Facts On File, 1991), 118.
119. *World War II: Day by Day*, 307.
120. *America at War: World War II*, 164.
121. Ibid.
122. *Hiroshima*, 45.
123. Ibid., 51.
124. *The Prince*, 13.
125. *The American Heritage Picture History of World War II*, 591.
126. *Hiroshima*, 64–65.

127. Sterling Mace and Nick Allen, *Battle-Ground Pacific: A Marine Rifleman's Combat Odyssey in K/3/5* (New York: St. Martin's Griffin, 2012), 213.
128. Yale Law School, The Avalon Project, "Atlantic Charter," accessed February 9, 2015. avalon.law.yale.edu/wwii/atlantic.asp.
129. Maurice Isserman, *America at War: The Korean War* (New York: Facts On File, 1992), 7.
130. Ibid., 36.
131. Gordon Cucullu, *Separated at Birth: How North Korea Became the Evil Twin* (Guilford: The Lyons Press, 2004), 82.
132. Ibid., 40–41.
133. The over fifty thousand deaths usually reported during the Korean war include all military deaths anywhere for any reason while the Korean conflict was ongoing. Battlefield deaths in Korea are reported at over thirty-three thousand. DoD numbers.
134. *America at War: The Korean War*, 69.
135. *Separated at Birth*, 71.
136. *Korea Reborn: A Grateful Nation Honors War Veterans for 60 Years of Growth* (Remember My Service Productions, 2013), 142.
137. *Separated at Birth*, 164.
138. *On War*, 185.
139. *America at War: The Korean War*, 74.
140. *Separated at Birth*, 75.

141. Soon Ok Lee, *Eyes of the Tailless Animals: Prison Memoirs of a North Korean Woman* (Bartlesville: Living Sacrifice Book Company, 1999), 9.
142. A special thank-you to Ron Burbridge for allowing me to interview him and for sharing his story of which this is but a small outline. He truly is an American hero.
143. A primary source for the historical background of Vietnam is:

    Maurice Isserman, *America at War: The Vietnam War* (New York: Facts on File, 1992).
144. Ibid., 13.
145. Ibid., 11.
146. Ibid., 20.
147. James Arnold and Gordon Rottman, *The Tet Offensive and The Siege of Khe Sanh* (Oxford: Osprey Publishing Ltd., 2006), 8.
148. *America at War: The Vietnam War*, 74–75.
149. *The Tet Offensive and The Siege of Khe Sanh*, 56.
150. Ibid., 57.
151. Ibid., 83–84.
152. Ibid., 85.
153. Ibid., 88–89.
154. Gary Williams, *Seal of Honor: Operation Red Wings and the Life of Lt. Michael P. Murphy, USN* (Annapolis: Naval Institute Press, 2010), 116.

155. "The National Security Strategy of the United States of America September 2002," accessed February 25, 2015. www.state.gov/documents/organization/63562.pdf., 9.
156. Ibid., Introduction.
157. Ibid., 6.
158. Marcus Luttrell with Patrick Robinson, *Lone Survivor: The Eyewitness Account of Operation Redwing and the Lost Heroes of Seal Team 10* (New York: Back Bay Books, 2007), 69.
159. *Seal of Honor*, 129.
160. *Lone Survivor*, 37.
161. *Seal of Honor*, 86.
162. *Lone Survivor*, 28.
163. Ibid., 31.
164. Ibid., 237.
165. *Seal of Honor*, 70.
166. *Lone Survivor*, 341.